the fading of the flesh
and the
flourishing of faith

SERIES EDITORS
Joel R. Beeke & Jay T. Collier

Interest in the Puritans continues to grow, but many people find the reading of these giants of the faith a bit unnerving. This series seeks to overcome that barrier by presenting Puritan books that are convenient in size and unintimidating in length. Each book is carefully edited with modern readers in mind, smoothing out difficult language of a bygone era while retaining the meaning of the original authors. Books for the series are thoughtfully selected to provide some of the best counsel on important subjects that people continue to wrestle with today.

the fading of the flesh
and the
flourishing of faith

George Swinnock

Edited by
J. Stephen Yuille

Reformation Heritage Books
Grand Rapids, Michigan

The Fading of the Flesh and the Flourishing of Faith
© 2009 by Reformation Heritage Books

Published by
Reformation Heritage Books
3070 29th St. SE
Grand Rapids, MI 49512
616-977-0889
e-mail: orders@heritagebooks.org
website: www.heritagebooks.org

Printed in the United States of America
22 23 24 25 26/12 11 10 9 8 7 6 5

Originally published—London, 1662

Special thanks to Encyclopedia Puritannica for supplying an
electronic version of the original text.

Library of Congress Cataloging-in-Publication Data

Swinnock, George, 1627-1673.
  The fading of the flesh and the flourishing of faith / George
Swinnock ; edited by J. Stephen Yuille.
      p. cm. — (Puritan treasures for today)
    ISBN 978-1-60178-072-0 (pbk. : alk. paper) 1. Christian life—
Puritan authors. I. Yuille, J. Stephen, 1968- II. Title.
  BV4501.3.S97 2009
  248.4'859—dc22
                                        2009040652

---

*For additional Reformed literature, request a free book list
from Reformation Heritage Books at the above address.*

Table of Contents

Preface

Several decades ago, John Piper coined a phrase that has become the impetus for countless individuals, ministries, organizations, and churches throughout the world. It is simply this: "God is most glorified in us when we are most satisfied in Him."[1] According to Piper, our problem is not that we desire pleasure, but that we do not desire it enough. The Psalmist declares, "In thy presence is fullness of joy; at thy right hand there are pleasures forevermore" (Ps. 16:11). In other words, God is our greatest pleasure. When we delight in Him, we demonstrate His excellence and, in so doing, declare His glory.

By his own admission, Piper drinks from a stream that extends all the way back to Augustine:

> How sweet did it suddenly become to be without the delights of trifles! And what at one time

---

1. John Piper, *Desiring God: Meditations of a Christian Hedonist* (Sisters: Multonomah Press, 1996).

I feared to lose, it was now a joy to me to put
away. For Thou didst cast them away from me,
Thou true and highest sweetness [some trans-
late this *sovereign joy*]. Thou didst cast them
away, and instead of them didst enter in Thyself,—sweeter than all pleasure, though not
to flesh and blood; brighter than all light, but
more veiled than all mysteries; more exalted
than all honour, but not to the exalted in their
own conceits.[2]

Over the centuries, many others have stooped to
drink from this same stream. Among them, the English
Puritans are particularly noteworthy, for they embraced
Augustine's "sovereign joy" in a fashion unlike any group
in the history of the church. The father of English
Puritanism, William Perkins, set the tone by defining
theology as "the science of living blessedly forever."[3] His
conviction was given creedal sanction in the first question of the *Westminster Shorter Catechism*: "What is the
chief end of man? Man's chief end is to glorify God, and
to enjoy Him forever." Subsequent Puritans continued to

---

2. Augustine, *Confessions*, trans. J. G. Pilkington, in *Nicene
and Post-Nicene Fathers*, 1:129 (IX:1).

3. William Perkins, *A Golden Chain; or, The description of
theology containing the order and causes of salvation and damnation,
according to God's Word*, in *The Works of William Perkins* (London,
1608), I:11.

express this same conviction. "God enjoyed is man's happiness."[4] "God is that supreme good, in the enjoyment of whom all true happiness lies."[5] "It is not every good that makes man blessed, but it must be the supreme good, and that is God."[6] "Man's happiness stands in his likeness to God, and his fruition of God."[7] "Every soul that hath a title to this rest, doth place his chief happiness in God. This rest consisteth in the full and glorious enjoyment of God."[8]

To a man, the Puritans believed that God designed us for a specific *end*—namely, to find pleasure in Him. They found the framework for their view in Aristotle, who penned, "There is some end (*telos*) of the things we do, which we desire for its own sake." This "end" is "the chief good" (happiness), which is "always desirable

---

4. Robert Harris, *The Way of True Happiness, Delivered in Twenty-four Sermons upon the Beatitudes* (1653; rpt., Morgan: Soli Deo Gloria, 1998), 18.

5. John Flavel, *The Works of John Flavel* (London: W. Baynes and Son, 1820; rpt., London: Banner of Truth, 1968), V:210.

6. Thomas Watson, *The Beatitudes: An Exposition of Matthew 5:1–12* (1660; rpt., Edinburgh: Banner of Truth, 1994), 29.

7. William Gurnall, *The Christian in Complete Armour: A Treatise of the Saints' War against the Devil* (1662–1665; London: Blackie & Son, 1864; rpt., Edinburgh: Banner of Truth, 1995), I:415.

8. Richard Baxter, *The Practical Works of Richard Baxter: Select Treatises* (London: Blackie & Son, 1863; rpt., Grand Rapids: Baker Book House, 1981), 54.

in itself and never for the sake of something else."[9] For Aristotle, the conclusion was primarily ethical; that is, the happy man is the virtuous man—virtue being the mean between two extremes. The Puritans, however, while embracing Aristotle's teleological framework, rejected his view of the virtuous man. They made it abundantly clear that man's "chief good" is God!

The Puritan George Swinnock stood firmly in this tradition. He was born in 1627 at Maidstone, Kent. He was a graduate of Cambridge (B.A.) and Oxford (M.A.). He was a pastor at St. Mary's chapel in Rickmansworth, Hertfordshire; then at St. Nicholas' chapel in Great Kimble, Buckinghamshire. Upon his ejection from the Church of England for nonconformity in 1662,[10] he entered the household of Richard Hampden to minister as family chaplain.[11] With the easing of political restrictions in 1672, he returned to his home of Maidstone to

---

9. Aristotle, *Nicomachean Ethics in The Works of Aristotle: Vol. IX*, ed. W. D. Ross (Oxford: Oxford University Press, 1963), I:2, 4, 7.

10. In 1662, Parliament passed an Act of Uniformity according to which all who had not received Episcopal ordination had to be re-ordained by bishops. Ministers had to declare their consent to the entire Book of Common Prayer and their rejection of the Solemn League and Covenant. As a result, approximately 2,000 ministers left the Church of England.

11. Richard Hampden was the father of John Hampden—famous for his support of the parliamentary forces during the English Civil War.

become pastor. He occupied this position for less than a year, dying at the age of forty-six.[12] Other than these few details, very little is known of him. Thankfully, however, his collected works are available to us.[13]

In the treatise before you, *The Fading of the Flesh and the Flourishing of Faith*, Swinnock affirms that man can only be satisfied by that which is accommodated to his nature. This necessarily means that man can only be satisfied by God. Why? First, God is perfect: "That which makes man happy must not have any want or weakness in it. It must be able to protect him against all evil and provide him with all good" (p. 90). Second, God is suitable: "It is an unquestionable truth that nothing can give true comfort to man except that which has a relation and bears a proportion to his highest and noblest part—his immortal soul" (p. 99). Third, God is eternal: "The soul cannot enjoy any perfection of happiness unless it is proportionate to its own duration" (p. 101). In a word, man can only find happiness in that which is suited to his soul. This means that he can only find happiness in God. Swinnock declares, "The excellence of the object

---

12. See *Dictionary of National Biography*, ed. S. Lee (London: Smith, Elder & Co., 1909).

13. You will find them in *The Works of George Swinnock*, 5 vols., ed. James Nichol (London, 1868; rpt., Edinburgh: Banner of Truth, 1992). Nichol's edition contains all of Swinnock's treatises except *The Life and Death of Mr. Thomas Wilson, Minister of Maidstone, in the County of Kent, M.A.* (London, 1672).

that we embrace in our hearts determines the degree of
our happiness. The saint's choice is right—God alone is
the soul's center and rest" (pp. 88–89). Having identified
God as man's satisfaction, Swinnock reminds us: "your
happiness depends entirely upon your taking the blessed
God for your utmost end and chiefest good" (p. 122).
Here, he clearly demonstrates his affinity with Augustine, whom he quotes as saying, "Lord, Thou hast made
our heart for Thee, and it will never rest till it come to
Thee; and when I shall wholly cleave to Thee, then my
life will be lively" (p. 146).

It is important to note that this "cleaving" to God
as our "utmost end" and "chief good" is not some empty
philosophical speculation on Swinnock's part. In his
"Epistle Dedicatory," addressed to "the courteous Mrs.
Jane Swinnock," he mentions that the "substantial part"
of this treatise was originally preached at the funeral for
Jane's husband, Caleb (Swinnock's cousin). He informs
her that God is teaching her "two lessons" through
her loss. First, "That your affections be taken off from
earthly possessions. Dying relations call for dying affections." Second, "That you choose the good part that shall
never be taken from you. Man's heart will be fixed on
somewhat as its hope and happiness. God therefore puts
out our candles, takes away relations, that we may look
up to the Sun, and esteem him our chiefest portion."[14]

---

14. Swinnock, *Works*, III:404–405.

This context is extremely significant, for it confirms that Swinnock's "sovereign joy" is not some idle speculation, but a personal and pastoral reality. In good and bad, prosperity and adversity, life and death, God alone is our portion!

With all that said, I unreservedly commend *The Fading of the Flesh and the Flourishing of the Faith* to you as rich food for the soul. Here, Swinnock is at his best, as he exhorts saint and sinner alike to delight in the One, who is "the sweetest love, the richest mercy, the surest friend, the chiefest good, the greatest beauty, the highest honour, and fullest happiness" (pp. 131–132).

J. Stephen Yuille
Glen Rose, Texas
September 2009

CHAPTER 1

Psalm 73 in Context

Holy Scripture is more famous than all other writings, because of its truthfulness. The books of men are like their bodies, prone to many weaknesses. After careful editing, they still contain errors. However, Holy Scripture is like God: full (without imperfection) and faithful (without corruption). Its author is the God of truth, for whom it is impossible to lie. Therefore, its matter must be the word of truth (Ps. 119:142; Titus 1:2; 2 Peter 1:21).

Among all the books of Scripture, the Psalms are most famous for their variety. Other books are historical, doctrinal, or prophetical, but the book of Psalms is all of these. It describes the history of the church, foretells the passion and resurrection of Christ, and declares the duty of a Christian. The Psalms, says one commentator, are a jewel, consisting of the gold of doctrine, the pearl of comfort, and the gem of prayer.

Psalm 73 is entitled *A Psalm of Asaph* or *A Psalm for Asaph.* Asaph was a prophet (2 Chron. 29:30) and musician (1 Chron. 15:19). As for its content, Psalm 73 consists of two parts. The first describes the godly man's trial: the grievous conflict between the Spirit and the flesh (vv. 1–15). The second describes the godly man's triumph: the glorious conquest of the Spirit over the flesh (vv. 16–28).

At the root of this conflict is envy. "I was," declares the psalmist, "envious at the foolish" (Ps. 73:3).

1. The Cause of the Psalmist's Envy

The psalmist's heart is troubled, because he sees the prosperity of the wicked (Ps. 73:3). Their prosperity is like weeds that infest the ground, are watered plentifully, and grow exceedingly, while good corn is thin and lean. It is like the lion and raven, unclean creatures that are spared, while the innocent lamb and dove are sacrificed. It is inconceivable to the psalmist that the wicked should flourish like the bay-tree, enjoy a constant spring and summer, and be fresh and green all year round, while the saints, like good apple trees, have their autumn and winter. This grieves him deeply. His sore eyes cannot behold the glorious sunshine of the wicked's prosperity.

2. The Cure for the Psalmist's Envy

In simple terms, the psalmist's disease is poor eyesight. An envious eye is an evil eye (Matt. 20:15). The remedy for such an ailment is a glimpse of the wicked's end: eternal misery. It is to see that they climb the ladder, like criminals, to the gallows for execution. This realization satisfies the psalmist.

Unbelievers ascribe envy to many causes. Some naturalists ascribe it to the principles of generation and corruption. The stoics ascribe it to the necessary connection of second causes. The astrologers ascribe it to the motion and influence of the stars, trying to show us the very houses of prosperity and adversity. The wiser among them, although their foolish hearts are still darkened, ascribe it to the will of Jupiter, who has vessels of good and bad things from which he gives to all people according to his pleasure. As for the removal of envy, unbelievers prescribe many cures. However, their medicines only serve to stir this disease. Their remedies are all kitchen medicine, such as grows in nature's garden. The real remedy must be fetched from afar.

I confess that the master of moral philosophy (Seneca), whom I most admire from among all the moralists, seems to touch on the same theme as the psalmist. Those says he, whom God approves and loves, are afflicted. Those, whom God seems to spare, are reserved for future suffering. Although there are many excellent insights in the moralist's work, he falls well short of Christianity. His sight is not good enough to look into the other world to behold the eternal pain of the wicked and the eternal pleasure of the good. However, it is this very vision that calms the storm in the psalmist's heart.

He sees that the wicked are not spared; their punishment is simply delayed.

The remedy that calms the boisterous waves, which threatens to swallow up the soul of the psalmist, is the different destinies of the saint and sinner. By faith, he foresees that the wicked man's whole life is but a tragedy. Although its start might be cheerful, its end is sorrowful. Although his power on earth is great for a time, yet his portion is in the lowest hell for all eternity. "Until I went into the sanctuary of God; then understood I their end. Surely thou didst set them in slippery places: Thou castedst them down into destruction. How are they brought into desolation, as in a moment! They are utterly consumed with terrors" (Ps. 73:17–19). The wicked are exalted, as the shellfish by the eagle, to be thrown down on some rock and devoured. Their most glorious prosperity is like a rainbow, which shows itself for a little time in all its flashy colors, and then vanishes. The Turks, considering the unhappy end of their officials, use this proverb, "He who is in the greatest office, is but a statue of glass." Wicked men walk on glass or ice. "Thou didst set them in slippery places." Suddenly, their feet slip. They fall, and break their necks. Oh, the sad reckoning that awaits them after all their merry meetings! Although their expensive food goes down pleasantly here, yet it rises in their stomachs later.

The psalmist also sees that the saints, after their short storm, enjoy an everlasting calm. "Thou shalt guide me with thy counsel, and afterward receive me to glory" (Ps. 73:24). Like the pillar of fire by night and cloud by day, Thou, my God, wilt march before me and direct me through the wilderness of this world, until I come to Canaan!

3. The Psalmist's Response

The above remedy leads the psalmist to declare to God, "Whom have I in heaven but thee? And there is none upon earth that I desire beside thee" (Ps. 73:25). Ungodly people may abound in sensual pleasures, but I have an infinitely better portion. They have the streams, which run pleasantly for a season, but will soon dry up. On the other hand, I have the fountain, which runs over and runs forever. They, like grasshoppers, skipping up and down on the earth, have their songs. Nevertheless, what tune may I sing? I am mounting up to heaven to enjoy God, who is unspeakably more desirable than anything is in either heaven or earth!

CHAPTER 2

Psalm 73:26 Explained

The psalmist declares, "My flesh and my heart faileth: but God is the strength of my heart, and my portion forever" (Ps. 73:26). As for this text, I will explain its terms and declare its doctrinal truths.

1. The Terms
"My flesh and my heart faileth me…"

1. Spiritual Sense
Some expositors interpret this statement in a spiritual sense. Among those who do, there is a difference of opinion.

First, some interpret it in an evil sense. They think the statement is a confession of the psalmist's former sin, and is related to the struggle between the flesh and the Spirit, mentioned at the beginning of the Psalm. It is as if the psalmist said, "I was so overwhelmed by self-conceit that I presumed to judge divine actions according to human reason, and to judge the stick under the water to be crooked, by the eye of my sense, when indeed it was straight. However, I now see that my flesh is not fit to judge in matters of faith, that neither my flesh nor my heart can grasp God's ways with men, and that I cannot hold out under Satan's temptations. If God had not supported me, my flesh would have utterly supplanted me." "My flesh and my heart faileth: but God is the strength of my heart" (Ps. 73:26). At times, the term *flesh* refers to corrupt human nature (Gal. 5:13). Why? (1) It is propagated by the flesh (John 3:6). (2) It is executed by the flesh (Rom. 7:25). (3) It is nourished, strengthened, and increased by the flesh (1 John 2:16).

Second, some interpret the statement in a good sense. They do not think it refers back to the beginning of the Psalm, but to the preceding verse: "Whom have I in heaven but thee? And there is none upon earth that I desire beside thee" (Ps. 73:25). These expositors affirm that the psalmist, having passionately fixed his heart on God as the most pleasant object in heaven and earth, was so overcome with vehement longing that he was ready to fade away. His spirit was ready to expire, because of the exuberance of his love to, and longing after, the blessed God. The weak cask of his body was ready to break, for it was not able to hold that strong and spiritual wine. "My flesh and my heart faileth." It is as if he says, "I am so ravished with delight in, and so enlarged in desire for, this infinitely beautiful object, that there is no more

spirit left in me. I am sick! If God does not appear, then
the strength of my heart will die out of love for Him!"

2. *Civil Sense*

Some expositors interpret the statement—"my flesh and
my heart faileth me"—in a civil sense. They affirm that
it refers to the psalmist's sufferings. He had a good rod
instead of a good piece of bread for his breakfast every
morning. The table was covered with sackcloth, and furnished with bitter herbs both at lunch and at supper.
"For all the day long have I been plagued, and chastened
every morning" (Ps. 73:14). The weight of this burden
was so great, crushing his body and oppressing his mind,
that—apart from God's almighty power—it would have
broken his back; his flesh and his heart would have
failed him.

3. *Natural Sense*

Some expositors interpret the statement in a natural
sense. According to this view, the psalmist is neither
referring to his fault (spiritual sense) nor his fear (civil
sense), but his frailty. It is as if he says, "My moisture
consumes, my strength abates, my flesh falls, and my
heart fails. Before long, my breath will be corrupt, my
days extinct, and the grave ready for me. How happy am
I, therefore, in having God for the strength of my heart!"
I take the words in this sense, as being most suitable to
the context.

"But God is the strength of my heart…"

These words mean that, although my flesh fails me, the Father of spirits does not fail me. When I am sinking, He will place His everlasting arm under me to save me. The Hebrew expresses it like this: "But God is the rock of my heart." In other words, He is a sure, strong, and immoveable foundation to build upon. Although the winds may blow and the waves may beat, when the storm of death comes, I have no reason to fear that the house of my heart will fall, for it stands upon a sure foundation: "God is the rock of my heart."

The strongest child of God is unable to stand alone. Like ivy, he needs something to support him, or else he falls to the ground. Of all seasons, the Christian has most need of support at his dying hour. At that time, he takes his leave of all his comforts on earth, and he encounters the sharpest conflicts from hell. Therefore, it is impossible for him to hold out without extraordinary help from heaven. The psalmist had armor ready to encounter his last enemy. He was a weak and fearful child, yet he was able to walk through the dark entrance of death, taking his Father by the hand. "Yea, though I walk through the valley of the shadow of death, I will fear no evil: for thou art with me" (Ps. 23:4). Although my heart is ready to fail me through the troubles of my life and at the trial of my death, I have a strong remedy that will cheer me in my saddest condition: "God is the strength of my heart."

"And my portion…"

This expression is a metaphor, taken from the ancient Jewish custom of dividing inheritances, whereby every one received his allotted portion. It is as if the psalmist says, "God is not only my rock to defend me from those storms that assault me, but He is my portion to meet all my needs and give me the fruition of all good." Some people have their portion on this side of the land of promise, but the author of all portions is the substance of my portion. My portion does not lie in the rubbish, as it does for those whose portion is in this life. My portion contains Him whom the heavens, and heaven of heavens, can never contain. God is the strength of my heart and my portion forever—not for a year, or an age, or a million ages, but for eternity!

Earthly portions are like roses, in that the fuller they blossom, the sooner they shed. They are often misused through pride and wasted through carelessness. Death always rends people and their portions asunder. However, my portion will always be full (without diminution) and first (without alteration). This God will be my God forever. He will be my guide and help until death. Even death, which dissolves so many bonds and unties close knots, will never separate me from my portion. On the contrary, it will give me a perfect and everlasting possession of it.

2. The Doctrines

Psalm 73:26 branches into two parts. First, there is the psalmist's complaint: "My flesh and my heart faileth." Second, there is the psalmist's comfort: "but God is the strength of my heart, and my portion forever." We may express it as follows: (1) there is the fading of his flesh—"My flesh and my heart faileth"; and (2) there is the flourishing of his faith—"but God is the strength of my heart, and my portion for ever."

From these two parts of the text, I will draw out two doctrinal truths. (1) Man's flesh will fail him. The highest and holiest man's heart will not hold out forever. The psalmist was great and gracious, yet his flesh failed him. (2) It is the comfort of a Christian, in his saddest condition, that God is his portion. This strong water kept the psalmist from fainting when his flesh and heart failed him.

CHAPTER 3

Man's Flesh Will Fail Him

I begin with the first doctrine: man's flesh will fail him. Those whose spirits are noble, will find their flesh to be brittle. The psalmist was great, but death made little of him. This cannon hits the great commanders as well as the common soldiers. Like a violent wind, it plucks up by the roots, not only low trees, but also tall cedars. Those who lie in beds of ivory must lie down in beds of earth. Some letters are made with large flourishes, but they are still ink like all the others. Some men have great titles—worshipful or honorable—but they are meaningless to death. They are moving earth and dying dust, just like ordinary men. Worship, honor, excellency, highness, and majesty, must all do homage to the scepter of this king of terrors.

When Constantius had entered Rome in triumph, and had stood a long time admiring the gates, arches, turrets, temples, theaters, and other magnificent buildings, at last he asked Hormisda what he thought of the place. "I take no pleasure in it at all," said Hormisda, "for

I see the end of this city will be the same as all her pre-decessors." What he said of places is as true of persons. Although men may admire them for a while, the state-liest and greatest buildings of their bodies will fall to the ground as their ancestors' bodies did before them (Job 3:15). This storm will beat on the prince's court as much as on the peasant's cottage. "What man is he that liveth, and shall not see death? Shall he deliver his soul from the hand of the grave? Selah" (Ps. 89:48). The psalm-ist challenges the whole world to find a person that can procure protection against death's arrest.

The psalmist was gracious, but grace gave way to nature. Death will, like hail and rain, fall on the best gardens as well as the wide wilderness. The wheat is cut down and carried into the barn; so are the tares. A godly man is free from the sting, but not from the stroke; from the curse, but not from the cross of death. Holy Hezekiah was able to extend his life for a few years (2 Kings 20:1–6). He obtained a reprieve for fifteen years, but not a pardon. The best fruit will perish, because it is worm-eaten. Both the gold and dross (the good and bad) go into this fire—the former to be refined, and the latter to be consumed.

"The voice said, 'Cry.' And he said, 'What shall I cry?' All flesh is grass, and all the goodliness thereof is as the flower of the field. The grass withereth, the flower fadeth: because the Spirit of the Lord bloweth upon it: Surely the people is grass" (Isa. 40:6–7). (1) These verses point to man's mortality. He is grass, withering grass—a flower, a fading flower. (2) These verses point to the certainty of death. "The voice said, 'Cry.'" In other words, the prophet received a charge from God to proclaim, "The people are grass!" (3) These verses point to the universality of death. The flesh of kings and counselors, the flesh of saints and martyrs, the flesh of high and low, the flesh of rich and poor—"All flesh is grass." Man is sometimes compared to the flower for its beauty, but here for its frailty. A flower will quickly fade. If it is not picked by the hand or cut down by an instrument of iron, the gentle breeze will quickly blow its beauty away.

Naturalists tell us of a flower called *ephemeron*, because it lasts but a day. Man is such a flower. His life is but a day, whether longer or shorter—a summer's or winter's day. How quickly the shadows of the evening stretch themselves upon him, and make it night! Pliny speaks of a golden vine that never withers. One day, the bodies of saints will be like that. However, at present, the best herbs, along with the worst weeds, wither. Neither the dignity of a prince nor the piety of a prophet can dissuade this enemy. Against this arrest, there is no bail.

By way of further explanation, I will lay down two or three reasons for the doctrine. Then, I will proceed to that which is practical.

1. Man's Corruptibility
The first reason for the doctrine is man's corruptibil-

ity. His body is called a house of clay (Job 4:19) and an earthly tabernacle (2 Cor. 5:1). The body of man is at best a clod of clay, curiously made and molded. The Greek proverb has a truth in it: "Man is but an earthen vessel." Some are more painted than others are in regard to dignity and place. Some are stronger vessels than the rest in regard of purity of constitution. However, all are earthen! "Verily every man at his best state is altogether vanity" (Ps. 39:5). All *Adam* is all *Abel*. Every man, when most high in regard of his hopes and most firm in regard of his foundation, is even then next door to corruption.

What the great apostle says in a proper sense, everyone may say in a common sense, "I die daily" (1 Cor. 15:31). We carry our curse around with us every moment. Against some people, it appears in the open field, often skirmishing with them. Against other people, it lies in ambush, waiting for an opportunity to fall on them and destroy them. In the healthiest bodies, it is as fire raked under the ashes, reserved for another day when it will ignite and burn.

God does not need to bring out His great artillery to knock down the building of man's body. A small touch will suffice. It is decaying all the time, and will eventually fall by itself. There is rottenness at the core of the fairest fruits. Our flesh is no match for the Father of spirits. An ordinary broom will sweep away the spider's web, because it has no stability despite its intricate weavings. As it was with the gourd of Jonah, so it is with the children of men: we breed and feed those worms that will devour and destroy us (Jonah 4:6–7). Every man's death toll hangs in his own steeple.

2. God's Fidelity

The second reason for the doctrine is God's fidelity. The righteous and gracious God has threatened eternal pains to the wicked as the wages of their sins, and He has promised endless pleasures to the godly as the reward of Christ's sufferings. Now, the place of payment, where these threats and promises will be accomplished, is the other world, to which death is the passage. Man dies, so that God's word may live. Man falls to the earth, so that God's truth may stand.

Sin is finite in regard of its subject, because it is the act of a limited creature. However, it is infinite in regard of its object, because it is committed against a boundless Creator. For this reason, it is punished with the absence of all good (which is an infinite loss) and with the presence of all evil (which is infinite in duration). The infernal pit is the place of those punishments, into which men descend by the ladder of death (Matt. 7:23; 25:41; Mark 9:49). Death is but the sinner's trap-door into hell. In England, criminals, guilty of a capital offense, are carried into a dungeon, and from there to the gallows. Similarly, ungodly men, who fail to plead for their pardon through the gospel, pass through the dungeon of death to the place of their dreadful and ever-lasting execution.

God has also determined to bestow an incomparable and unchangeable crown on the members of Christ. It is their Father's pleasure to give them a kingdom. Death is but the young prophet that anoints them for it, and gives them actual possession of it. They must put off their rags of mortality, so that they may put on their robes of glory. It is in the night of death that saints go to their blessed and eternal rest. The corn must first die before it can spring up fresh and green. Israel must die in Egypt before she can be carried into Canaan. There is no entrance into paradise but through the flaming sword of this angel, death, that stands at the gate. The soul must be delivered from the prison of the body, so that it may enjoy the glorious liberty of the sons of God. This bird of paradise will never sing merrily, nor sing the praises of its Maker perfectly, until it is freed from this cage.

The sinner dies, so that, according to God's Word, he may receive the bitter fruit of his evil ways. Death is to him as the gate through which condemned criminals pass to their deserved destruction. The saint dies, so that, according to God's promise, he may enjoy the purchased possession. Death to him is as the dirty lane through which Chrysostom passed to a feast—a dark, short way by which he goes to the marriage supper of the Lamb. His body is mortal, so that his sins and sufferings may not be immortal.

3. Man's Apostasy

The third reason for the doctrine is man's apostasy. Death broke in upon man by virtue of the fact that man broke God's commands. We would never have fallen to dust, if we had not first fallen from our duties. Sickness would never have seized our bodies, if sin had not first seized our souls.

The Pelagians and Socinians say that death is not a consequence of sin, but a condition of nature. However, the God of truth ascribes the origin of death to Adam's desire to be like Him (Gen. 3:15; Rom. 5:12). As insensibility in the head diffuses malignity throughout the whole body, thereby corrupting and destroying it, even so the fruit, that Adam ate, contained poison that entered into his being. Its venom is transmitted, like Gehazi's leprosy, to his seed (2 Kings 5:27). Some tell us that Adam would often turn his face toward the Garden of Eden and weep, reflecting upon what he had done. I am certain he had reason to do so, for we all received the infection from him. It is through him that the whole world is tainted and turned into a pest house. Whatever delight he derived from the act was nothing in comparison to the result: death.

It seems unquestionable that man, in his state of innocence, had a conditional, although not absolute, immortality. He was mortal, in that he was made of corruptible elements. However, he was immortal, in that he was free from the law of death by virtue of the covenant.

Before the Fall, he had a possibility of not sinning. After the Fall, he has a necessity of sinning. Likewise, in his state of innocence, he had a possibility of not dying, and, in his state of apostasy, he has a necessity of dying. If he had stood, he would have been translated, like Enoch, without seeing death (Gen. 5:21–24). He would have entered his Father's house without walking through the dark doorway of death.

The flesh fails us, because sin has defiled it. Man's flesh was overcome with pride. Since then, it has been liable to putrefaction (Ps. 90:7). Sin is called "a body of death," because it causes the death of the body (Rom. 7:24). When asked who set up the stately buildings in Rome, it was answered, "the sins of Germany," meaning the money that the pope's agents received for pardons granted to the Germans. If you ask, "Who tears down the building of man's body," I answer, "the sins of man." Sin turns such costly, beautiful houses into confused, ruinous heaps.

Draco, the lawgiver, appointed death as the punishment for every offense. For this reason, his laws are said to be written in blood. When asked why, he explained that, although it seemed unjust to make all crimes equal in punishment, it was actually a great demonstration of justice, for the least breach of the law deserves death. The light of nature teaches that sinners are worthy of death (Rom. 1:23). The condition of all sinners lies in the valley of the shadow of death.

CHAPTER 4

The Folly of Living for the Flesh

Having explained the first doctrine—that man's flesh will fail him—I will now speak of application. The doctrine is useful by way of instruction and exhortation.

First, by way of instruction: If man's flesh will fail him, then what fools are they whose primary concern is to feed and please the flesh! We laugh at the vanity and folly of children when we see them very busy and exerting so much effort in building houses of cards or pies of dirt. The majority of men are but children of larger dimensions. They are even more foolish, because they ought to be wiser. What is their main work? Is it not to make provision for the flesh, and to provide fuel for the fire of its covetousness and water for the leviathan of its sensuality and air for the chameleon of its ambition? They act as if God had no other design in sending them into the world than that they might be cooks to dress their bodies as well as possible for the worms.

Their chief care is, "What will we eat? What will we drink? What will we wear? How will we live in these costly and hard times?" As vermin in dunghills, they live and feed on such filth, never once asking their souls in earnest: "What will you do for the bread of heaven? How will you put on the robes of Christ's righteousness, so that your nakedness does not appear to your shame? What will you do to be saved, to live eternally?" These things do not occupy their thoughts. Like flies, they are overcome with the spirits of wine, and nourished with froth. They think it is enough that, when they come to die, they bequeath their souls to God in their wills. As a result, they devote their whole lives to the service of their bodies. Like dying men, they smell of earth, and carry its complexion in their very countenance.

If a man who had two houses in his possession—one belonging to him and one belonging to his landlord—were to neglect his own house and leave it to ruin while night and day mending and adorning his landlord's house as if he could never make it neat enough, would not everyone condemn this man as a fool or a madman? Truly, this is the very case with most men. The body is our house of clay, in which we are tenants at another's will. We may be turned out of its doors without so much as an hour's warning. However, the soul is our own everlasting possession. Yet, the immortal soul is slighted. No time is taken for a serious view of its wants. No cost is laid out for its supply. While men are plotting and studying to gratify and please their fading flesh, they treat their soul as if it does not matter whether it swims or sinks forever. Oh, this is one of the most lamentable sights that eyes can behold: the servant riding on horseback while the prince goes on foot!

It is reported of a certain philosopher that, when he was dying, he bequeathed a great sum of money to the man who was found to be most foolish. His executor travelled all over in search of the man who excelled all others in folly. At last, he came to Rome, where he found a consul, sentenced to death for abusing his office, and another man who cheerfully assumed the consul's office. The executor delivered the money to this man, informing him that he was the most foolish man in the world, for he had witnessed the miserable end of his predecessor, yet still joyfully succeeded him in his office. How much do most professing Christians resemble this foolish consul? They see their sensual companions, like sheep, feeding in their fleshly pastures, suddenly culled out by death. They see in the Word, if they believe God, the block on which these sheep are laid by that bloody butcher, Satan, and the knife that he runs up to the very haft in the throat of their precious souls. They see the heavy curse of the law and the infinite wrath of the Lord, which they must undergo forever. Yet, they are not frightened. On the contrary, they merrily follow these sheep to the place of endless mourning.

Reader, if you are one of these fleshpots of Egypt, then you are guilty of such folly and madness. Is not your spirit a heavenly plant, the immediate workmanship of the glorious God? Moreover, is not your flesh, like the first Adam, of the earth? Are you not a fool to prefer dirt to that which is divine? Is not your spirit the imprint and image of God Himself in its immortality, noble faculties, and capacity of honoring and enjoying His infinite majesty? Is not your body the resemblance of beasts? Are you not unwise in esteeming that which is brutish above that which is the picture of God's own perfections? Moreover, is not the wellbeing of your body involved in the welfare of your soul? As the branches depend upon the root for their flourishing, your body depends upon your soul for its salvation. How mad are you to let the vessel sink while presuming to preserve the passenger that sails in it! Will not the life of your soul run parallel with the life of God and the line of eternity? Has not God told you that your flesh will fail you? Do you not already find it now tottering and, as it were, telling you that it must soon fall down? Are you not a fool in the highest degree to place all your eternal happiness and to set all your stress and weight for your unchangeable estate upon a rotten branch that will certainly break under you, when you may have sure footing and lay up a good foundation by giving hearty attention to your heaven-born soul? Oh, consider it, and give conscience permission to call you a fool so that you may be wise forever! What wrong has your soul done to you that, to take vengeance upon it, you make its slave its sovereign?

Why do you make that part, by which you are kin to the beasts, the lord, and king of your soul?

The truth is that were not men drowned in sensuality (like those, according to Seneca, who do not know whether they stand or sit unless their slaves tell them) and their consciences seared and made senseless, it would be impossible for them to live for the flesh. Some cunning thieves, if there is a watchdog at the house they intend to rob, will give it some bits of food in order to keep it from barking while they plunder the house. Likewise, the devil has a way of making men's consciences dumb while he robs them of their inestimable souls. Poor foolish creatures! They are lazing on their beds of carnal security and delighting themselves in their dreams of lying vanities. In the meantime, the devil rifles their houses and takes away all that is of value! Yet, as fast as conscience is now asleep, it will shortly awaken, and then what fears will possess them! Oh, how clearly will they see their folly in sowing to the flesh and trusting in that which was never true to any! Then they will cry, "If we had served our souls as faithfully as we have served our flesh, they would not have failed us like this."

Friends, God Himself has given you this truth as the masterpiece of wisdom: Your flesh will fail you! "Hear counsel, and receive instruction, that thou mayest be wise in thy latter end" (Prov. 19:20). Perhaps you care for none of these things. It is death to you to think of death. You hate it, as Ahab did Micaiah, because it never speaks well of you (2 Chron. 18:7). Your voice to death is as Pharaoh's to Moses, "Get thee from me…see my face no more" (Ex. 10:28). You are resolved to riot and revel, and therefore you cannot endure to think of the day of reckoning. Well, put away the thoughts of it, as far and as much as you can! Make as light of it as your hardened heart will allow you! Yet, know this: It is on its way, hurling towards you with a warrant from the God of heaven for your execution! Oh, when you see its grim face, how will your heart tremble! When you hear its dreadful voice, how will your ears tingle! The flesh, which you now pamper, will then wax pale. The vessels, from which you now draw your comforts, will then run dry. Then, oh then, how mournfully will you cry out, "Oh pastors, oh teachers, the counsel which you gave me was of infinite weight and consequence, but I, fool, mad-man, had not the sense to follow it!"

I will conclude this use with a sad story that Athe-naeus tells of a great monarch's life and death, in which, as in a looking-glass, you may see that flesh-pleasing vanities will end in soul-piercing miseries and that, no matter how wise a man is regarded by the world, he is but a fool in his latter end. Ninus, the Assyrian mon-arch, had an ocean of gold and other riches—more than the sand in the Caspian Sea. He never stirred up the holy fire among the magi. He never touched his god with the sacred rod according to the law. He never offered sacri-fice, nor worshipped the deity, nor administered justice.

However, he was most diligent in eating and drinking. Ninus is now dead. Now, hear him speak: "At one time, I was Ninus. I drew the breath of a living man, but now I am nothing but clay. I have nothing, but what I ate. I have nothing, but what I lavished on myself in lust. That was and is all my portion. I have gone to hell. I have taken neither gold nor horse nor silver chariot with me. I, who wore a miter, am now a little heap of dust."

CHAPTER 5

Be Prepared to Die!

Knowing that man's flesh will fail him is also useful by way of exhortation. It runs in two distinct channels: partly to the sensual unbeliever and partly to the serious believer. I will begin by speaking two words to the former.

Since your flesh will fail you, you must mind the salvation of your soul. When one leaf falls in autumn, we conclude that all will soon follow. From the deaths of others, you ought to conclude that you too will die. When a man's lease of the house, in which he lives, is almost expired, he begins to look for another house, so that he will not be exposed to the wind and weather. Reader, I come to you with a message this day from the faithful God, and it is to inform you that the lease of your life is almost expired. The time of your departure is at hand. What house will you provide for your precious soul, so that it is not exposed to the roar of damned spirits and rage of tormenting devils? The Roman gladiators, resigned to death, were careful to carry themselves in such a manner that they might fall gallantly. I am certain that you are appointed for the dust. Oh, where is your care to die comfortably? Perhaps you are someone who has planned for your funeral—how your body is to be laid in the coffin. The finest sheets and clothes will adorn your clod of clay and cover your carcass, in order to entertain the worms at their feast. However, in the meantime, do you not have any thoughts of preparing your immortal soul for the coming of the bridegroom?

When you die, you make your final cast for your everlasting state. You are never allowed another cast. Where you dwell the night you die is your eternal home. A work that is of such infinite importance and that is done only once, must be done well. God has given you but one arrow to hit the mark. If you shoot it at random, He will never put another arrow in your quiver. God will not allow a second edition to correct the errors in the first. Therefore, it behooves you to consider with all seriousness what happens when you die.

One would think that you would take little comfort in any creature while your eternal state is in such danger. Augustine wondered at the Roman citizen who could sleep quietly when he had a great debt to pay. What rest can you have, and what delight can you enjoy, when you owe such a vast amount to the infinite justice of God, and when He is determined to have full satisfaction either in this world or in the one to come? When David offered Barzillai the pleasures and preferment of his royal palace, Barzillai refused them, because he knew he was about to die. "How long have I to live, that I should go up with the king unto Jerusalem?... Let thy servant, I pray thee, turn back again, that I may die" (2 Sam. 19:34–37). In other words, "Do not court me! I have one foot in the grave. My glass is almost run out. Let me go home and die!" Without a doubt, you have even more reason to wink on these withering comforts and to commit yourself to a diligent preparation for death. The Thebans made a law that no man should build a house until he had first made his grave.

Every part of your life should remind you of your approaching death. The moralist (Seneca) speaks the truth: "You live by deaths." Your food is the dead carcasses of birds, fish, and animals. Your finest clothes are the worm's grave before they are your garments. Look up to the heavens. The sun rises and sets. Likewise, your life, which shines bright at present, will soon set. How much does it behoove you to do the work of Him who sent you into the world while it is still day (John. 9:4)? Look down to the earth. There, you see your mother, out of whose womb you came, and in whose bowels you will be laid. The dust and graves of others cry out to you, as Gideon to his soldiers, "Look on me, and do likewise" (Judg. 7:17). Oh, prepare your soul for that day!

If you rise up and walk in the streets, you see houses where men and women once lived. Behold, the places that once knew them know them no more. They are gone, and have carried nothing with them but their godliness or ungodliness. If you lie down, your sleep is the image of death. You do not know whether you will awake in a bed of feathers or a bed of flames. However, you do know that your body will soon lie down in the grave, and there remain until the resurrection. Look at your companions. You can see death sitting on their faces. It is creeping up on them in the deafness of their ears and in the dimness of their eyes. It is hurling towards them in the very height and zenith of their natural perfections. Look at your own house of clay. Perhaps death looks out your windows. It most certainly looks in your windows. You wear it on your face. You bear it in your bones. Does it not make sense to prepare for it? Oh, reader, a serious consideration of your death, that you are dust, would be very wholesome for your declining and decaying soul!

Hard bones, soaked in vinegar and ashes, grow so soft that they can be cut with a thread. Permit me to soak your hard heart for half an hour in such a mixture! It may so soften your heart, through the work of the Holy Spirit in the Word, that you become wise unto salvation. It is reported of a man, named Guerricus, that after hearing these words read in the church—"And all the days that Adam lived were nine hundred and thirty years: and he died...and all the days of Seth were nine hundred and twelve years: and he died...and all the days of Enos were nine hundred and five years: and he died...and all the days of Methuselah were nine hundred sixty-nine years: and he died" (Gen. 5:5–27) — he was so moved by the certainty of death that he devoted himself wholly to God. Friend, if you have an ounce of true love for your soul, and its unchangeable condition in the other world, the consideration of death will make a deep impression upon you.

In order to awaken and provoke you while there is still time and hope, and then to help and heal you, I offer you the following thoughts.

1. Death Is Near

First, do you not realize that death is certainly coming? As the young prophet said to Elisha, "Knowest thou that the Lord will take thy master from thy head today?" (2 Kings 2:3). Reader, do you know that the Lord will take your soul out of your body, and send it to the unknown regions of the other world, where you will see things that you have never seen, hear things that you have never heard, and understand things that you have never understood? Perhaps you will answer me, as Elisha did the young prophet, "Yea, I know it, hold ye your peace" (2 Kings 2:3). Nevertheless, I still urge you to consider death. Besides, I am certain that your knowledge of death is, as Cicero says of the Athenians, "like artificial teeth, for show only." You do not yet know it for your good. Therefore, permit me to impress it upon you.

Do you know that God will bring you to death, and to the house appointed for your eternal abode?

Do you know that your ruddy countenance will wax pale, your sparkling eyes will look ghastly, your warm blood will cool in your veins, your marrow will dry up in your bones, your skin will shrivel, your sinews will shrink, and your very heartstrings will crack? Moreover, have you ever prepared one moment for this hour? Do you not read in the writings of God that no man has power over the day of his death (Eccl. 8:8)? No man has power to resist death's force, or power to procure terms of peace. The greatest emperor, with the strength of all his subjects, cannot withstand death. The most eloquent orator, by his strongest reasons and most passionate expressions, cannot persuade death. The deepest counselor, by all his insight, cannot outsmart death.

There is no discharge from that war. Everyone must appear in person. There is no appearing by proxy. Even though the tenant may desire to stand for his landlord, or the subject for his sovereign, or the father for his child, as David for Absalom (2 Sam. 18:33), it will not be accepted. All must appear in the battlefield, and look that grim Goliath, death, in the face. "It is appointed unto men once to die" (Heb. 9:27). God has decreed it, and man cannot disannul it. The grammarian, as one smartly observes, can decline nouns in every case, yet can decline death in no case. Death is every moment shooting its arrows abroad in the world. Although it shoots above you, slaying your superiors, and below you, removing your inferiors, and on your right hand, killing your friends, and on your left hand, causing your acquaintances to drop, it will never cease shooting until it kills you. Your life may be preserved for a while, tossed from hazard to hazard, like a ball by the tennis rackets, yet it will eventually fall to the earth. When death, this son of a murderer, sin, comes to take away your head, there will be no one to shut the door or hold him back. Men that must travel, prepare for all weather. Oh, what a madman you are! You know that this enemy will certainly come, and that, when he does, he can both kill and damn, destroy both your body and soul, yet you take no care to prepare yourself for that hour!

In other matters, you provide for what may be. Will you not provide for what must be? In summer, you store fuel and food for winter. You work early and late to increase your provisions and add to your possessions, so that your children may enjoy them. Where is your sense in toiling for an uncertainty while foolishly neglecting what is of necessity?

2. Death May Come Suddenly

Second, do you realize that death may come suddenly? Some diseases no sooner appear, but we disappear. Death, like a flash of lightning, has suddenly burned down many bodies. It sometimes shoots white powder, executing without warning.

Pope Alexander choked on a fly. Anacreon, the poet, choked on a grape. Aeschylus was killed by the shell of a tortoise, which an eagle let fall on his bald head, mistaking it for a rock. A Duke of Brittany was crushed to death in a crowd. King Henry II of France was killed while jousting. I could name many others who took a shortcut to their long homes. Belshazzar, carousing in his wine, drunk his death (Dan. 5:30). Amnon, merry at a feast, met with death (2 Sam. 13:28–29). Korah and his companions find the earth opening her mouth and swallowing them up (Num. 16:30). Herod ends his proud speech, and immediately he is sent to the place of silence (Acts 12:20–23). Ananias and Sapphira finish their lies and their lives at the same time (Acts 5:4–10).

In scarce a week, there are those, in the places where we live, who are suddenly sent into the other world by violent or natural means. That which has happened to one man may happen to any man. Reader, you may talk, like the fool, of living many years when God, whose word must stand, says, "This night thy soul shall be required of thee" (Luke 12:20). Oh, what will then become of you? Your eternal condition, that state which is forever and ever, depends on this uncertain life. Are you not mad to be reveling and roaring, dallying and delaying, when your unchangeable state is in danger?

Thieves, after committing a robbery, frequently gather at taverns, where they drink joyfully and divide their spoil. Suddenly, the constable enters the room, ends all their celebrating, and arrests them. After the trial for their felonies, they are carted off to prison. Many sinners, in the midst of their carnal celebrations, have been hauled off to eternal torments. The philosophers say that the weather is milder before a snowfall. When the sky is most clear, then the greatest thunderstorm comes. Sodom had a sunshiny morning, but a storm of fire and brimstone before nightfall (Gen. 19:24). I assure you that you have nothing to excuse you in your greatest pleasures from such a sudden punishment. You are already a condemned person, and you lack nothing but the messenger—death. You lack nothing but a hurdle, horse, and halter to carry you to your deserved execution. "God shall shoot at them with an arrow; suddenly shall they be wounded" (Ps. 64:7). When the bird is sunning herself at the top of a tree, not even thinking about the hunter below, it is killed by a sudden shot.

Perhaps you trust in your youth and strength. Because you feel no infirmity, you do not fear mortality. You think that death only goes to the dead bones and dry breasts or to those who see with four eyes and walk on three legs. Do you not realize that death never observes the laws of nature? As young as you are, you may be rotten before you are ripe. Your sun may set at high noon. The Jews have a proverb: the old mule often carries the young mule's skin to the market. Blossoms are liable to nipping, as well as full-grown fruit to rotting. Have not people been married and buried in the same week? Have they not been dressed for their weddings and their coffins in the same day? "Boast not thyself of tomorrow; for thou knowest not what a day may bring forth" (Prov. 27:1).

Do you trust in your strength? Alas, the leviathan of death laughs at the shaking of that spear! He views your strength as straw and your youth as rotten wood. He makes a hole in a strong, new ship, and it sinks. Your body may be as strong as a fort, but death does not need to besiege it with lingering diseases. Death can undermine your body, and blow it down in a moment. Reason, therefore, with yourself: "This day may be the last day that I ever see. This hour may be the last hour that I ever live. These words may be the last words that I ever speak. Oh, what a fool am I to live without fear next door to the eternal fire! There is only one step between hell and me. For all I know, my next step may take me there. Then, I am gone forever! Surely, this realization should consume my carnal joy!

Death is called "war" (Eccl. 8:8). Orders may come from the Lord of hosts for your sudden march to war. You may not even have an hour's warning to put on your armor or prepare yourself. Invasions are far more dangerous than pitched battles, because they are sudden and take men unprepared. I must warn you that, whenever death comes, it will be dreadful and dangerous. It will surprise you and take you unprepared. You will be unable to make any resistance. Oh, how it will tear your soul, like a lion, rending it in pieces, because there will be no one to deliver you! Every enemy kills the one who goes about unarmed and naked. Death to a sinner is always sudden. They go down quickly into hell (Job 21:13).

3. Death Is Final

Third, do you realize that, whenever death comes, it will be too late to prepare for it? The ship must be rigged in the harbor, for it is too late to do it in the midst of a storm out on the ocean. You can delightfully spend your days without Christ and grace, but, when the bridegroom comes by death, you will, as the foolish virgins, seek oil, because your lamp will have gone out (Matt. 25:1–13). Then it will be too late! Only those who are ready will enter with Him. I have read of a woman in Cambridge, who, lying on her deathbed, was visited by people of worth and piety. She heard heavenly discourse from them. However, they heard nothing from her but this: "Call another time! Call another time!" However, time passes quickly. Once gone, it is irrecoverable. "Time," says Bernard "would be a good commodity to possess in hell if it could be purchased at any price." Oh, when you come to die, a week, a day, even an hour, will be more valuable to you than the entire world! But it will be impossible to delay death until another time. When death calls, ready or unready, willing or unwilling, you will not deny it. You will go to the place from which you will never return.

The tide will not hold back for the greatest merchant's goods. He must ship his goods before the tide or leave them behind. Death will not wait for any man to prepare his heart with grace. He must do it before death comes, or else he can never do it. If our spiritual change does not occur before our natural change (death), we will be unchangeably miserable. Petronius tells of a man, named Eumolpus, who, in a terrible storm, was composing poetry. When the ship hit a rock, and they told him to save himself, he answered, "Leave me alone until I have finished one verse." Death will not wait while you finish the greatest of works.

Reader, I do not doubt that, although you live as a slave to sin and Satan, you will want to die as the Lord's freeman. However, God warns you that if you live in bondage to your lusts, there is no liberty when you die (Eccl. 9:10). You must give attention to your soul and ensure your salvation right now. If not, it can never be done. You cannot do it in the place where you are going. Life is death's seedtime, and death is life's harvest. Expect a crop, both for quality and quantity, that is answerable to the seed that you sow at present! You cannot live with God in the hereafter unless you live for God here.

Friend, think seriously about it. Your preparation for death must be now or never. Bees work hard in summer, flying over fields, and sucking flowers, in order to make provision for winter, at which time no honey can be made. The shellfish takes in moisture while the tide flows over it. In so doing, it is supplied for the time when the waters ebb. Will you, like a drone, sleep now and starve later? Let your reason judge carefully. Is it a suitable time to prepare your soul for the marriage feast of the Lamb in the dark night of death? What can you possibly hope to do at that dismal hour? The day is gone, and your soul is lost, because you, unworthy wretch, deferred it until it was too late. Will you call to the sun of your life, as Joshua did (Josh. 10:12–13), "Stand still for one hour, so that I may take vengeance on these fleshly lusts, which keep me from heavenly Canaan"? Alas, alas, it will not listen to you! It cannot obey you, for time will be no more. You are entering eternity. Remember, you have been warned! Do not be like Caesar, who was warned by Artemidorus of the conspiracy to kill him, yet simply pocketed the warning, and went about greeting the people until he was indeed murdered.

CHAPTER 6

Further Reasons to Be Prepared to Die

4. Death Is a Trial

Fourth, do you realize that your dying hour will be a trying hour? When grapes arrive at the press, their worth is tested. The sailor's skill is seen in a storm. The soldier's courage is known when he enters combat. While he is in the garrison, he may boast of great things, but he is only fighting with his words. In a battle, all will see how he can handle his sword. Many, who boast when they know their enemy is far away, change their countenance when they meet him in the battlefield.

Perhaps you lie warm in your earthly comforts, with no enemy in sight. When this champion (at the sight of which the hearts of kings and captains have melted like snow before the sun) shows itself and offers to fight you for your soul, heaven, and happiness, then you will know what you are made of. You will know whether you have the faith and spirit of a David, who is able to face death in the Lord (Ps. 23:4). At present, you are a ship in the harbor and thereby are kept above water. However, when you launch into the ocean of death, the boisterous waves and tempestuous winds will soon discover your leaks, and show you what is lacking. It is as if you have some pieces of armor with which you hope to defend yourself against the strokes of death. Nevertheless, know that death will stab through all your paper shields of profession, privileges, and performances, if you are a stranger to Christ and the power of godliness.

Your life is like the lowering of a fisherman's net. Your death is like the raising of the net. While the net is lowered, a man cannot tell for certain what he will catch, for the net may break and the fish may escape. Similarly, while you live, your aim and end are not so evident. However, at your death, when the net is raised, then you will see what you have caught. At their deaths, godly men may look to the Lord of life, and say, "At Thy word we have lowered our nets and caught abundantly. We fished for holiness and caught happiness. We fished for grace and caught glory. We have fished for honor, and have caught immortality." However, it may be that, when the net of your life is raised, you will say, "Lord, I have fished all night, all my lifetime, and have caught nothing. I fished for honors, pleasures, and riches, and I have caught nothing but the weeds of wrath and damnation. I blessed myself many times, like the confident farmer, because of the good show that my corn made on the ground. But now the threshing time has arrived, and I find nothing but straw and chaff, vanity, and vexation."

Death will be a trying hour for two reasons.

1. Your Temporal Mercies Will Leave You

First, it will be a trying hour, because all your temporal mercies will leave you. When the hand of death shakes the tree of life, all the fair blossoms fall off. "For we brought nothing into this world, and it is certain we can carry nothing out" (1 Tim. 6:7). The hedgehog finds a pile of apples, and gathers as many as she can upon her prickles, but, when she returns to her burrow, she throws them all down and does not carry any in with her. Similarly, men walk in a vain shadow and disturb themselves in vain, heaping up riches that die with them. Naked they come into the world, and naked they leave the world. Plutarch wisely compares great men to counters, which one hour stand for thousands and the next hour stand for nothing. Hermocrates, unwilling that anyone should enjoy his estate after his death, made himself his own heir in his will. Athenaeus tells of a covetous man that, on his deathbed, swallowed several pieces of gold and sewed up others in his coat, commanding that they be buried with him. Who does not laugh at such folly?

In the storm of death, all your glory and riches, which you exerted so much effort in gathering, must be thrown overboard. As the great Sultan has an officer that searches everyone that enters his presence, in order to take away all their weapons, so the great God will search you by His messenger of death, and take away all your wealth. In that day, the crowns of princes and shackles of prisoners, the rags of beggars and scarlet of courtiers, the honors and offices of the highest, the meat, drink, sleep, and mirth of the lowest, must be set aside.

As it was said of Sarah, "It ceased to be with [her] after the manner of women" (Gen. 18:11), so the time will come when it will be said of you, "It ceases to be with him after the former manner." At present, you relish your food, delight in your friends, ravish your ears with melodious sounds and your eyes with beautiful sights, rejoice in things of no consequence, and entertain yourself with vain pursuits. However, when death comes, "It will cease to be with you after the former manner." At present, you please yourself in your lovely relations and pride yourself in your stately possessions. These weak props preserve your spirit from sinking at present. What will become of you when they are all taken away? What will become of you when you bid farewell forever to your wife, children, and friends? What will become of you when you say to your house, lands, possessions, sports, and pastimes, "Adieu for eternity"? What will become of you when you say, as dying Pope Adrian did, "Oh, my soul, the loving companion of my body, you are entering a solitary place, where you will never find anymore pleasure"? At the hour of death, your most costly jewels and most pleasing delights will be as the pearl in an oyster, not your privilege or perfection, but your disease and destruction.

When those carnal comforts are gone, your spiri-

tual comforts (if you have any) will be revealed. When
the hand that held you by the chin, keeping you above
water, is taken away, your skill in swimming will be
discovered. When the worth of those earthly delights,
which supported your spirits for a time, is spent, it will
appear whether nature has any strength.

2. Your Spiritual Enemies Will Assail You

Second, death will be a trying hour, because all your
spiritual enemies will assail you. Those adversaries,
which were once hidden, lurking out of sight, will appear
openly, and wound you to the very heart.

For starters, your sins will assault you. When the
prisoner appears before the judge, the evidence is produced, and the witnesses, which were unknown, show
themselves. When you go to stand before the judge of
the whole earth, your sins will accompany you. In the
night of death, those frightful ghosts will walk. Your
lusts, which are now lying dormant, will then be ram-
pant. You may say to death, as the woman to the prophet,
"Art thou come unto me to call my sin to remembrance,
and to slay my son?" (1 Kings 17:18). Are you come to
call my sins to remembrance, and to slay my soul?

While the hedgehog walks on land, she does not
seem to be too ugly, but, when she sprawls in the water,
her deformity appears. While men walk on earth, they
usually judge themselves fair, because they can find others who are fouler. However, death will remove their

masks and give them a mirror, in which all the spots, dirt, and wrinkles in the faces of their hearts and lives will be visible. Men often flatter themselves, but death never flatters anyone.

It is observable that Haman, the day he died, was named according to his character: "The adversary and enemy is this wicked Haman" (Esth. 7:6). In all likelihood, Haman had many titles given to him before this one. Some had called him "Haman the great," "Haman the magnificent," "Haman the prince," "Haman the virtuous." However, when he is about to die, it is "wicked Haman." At that time, he is called by his proper name. He had never heard his right name until that moment: "The adversary and enemy is this wicked Haman." It may be that, in your lifetime, you are called "great" or "gracious," because you occupy a place higher than others do. However, when death comes, those gaudy colors will be wiped away, and you will discover that you are not the King of heaven's favorite, but His fool.

At death, Satan will attack you with his biggest guns. When his time is short, his rage is greatest. This is his hour. When you, through pain of body and perplexity of mind, are least able to resist, then the devil will come with his fiercest assaults. If, on your deathbed, you should think of turning to God, Satan has a thousand ways to turn you away from such thoughts. When there is only one decisive battle for a kingdom, what fighting and striving there is! When the devil, who knows that you are already his, has but a few hours to wait for you, be assured that he will watch beside your sickbed night and day. If all the power of hell can prevent it, then medicine will not benefit your body and counsel will not benefit your soul.

Will it not be a trying hour when the cloth is drawn and your bodily comforts are all taken off the table? Will not death search you to the quick when those thieves (all your sins), in their frightening images, break in upon you? The elders of Samaria said of Jehu, when he sent for them to prepare to fight with him, "Two kings stood not before him, and how shall we?" (2 Kings 10:4). Adam and angels could not stand before sin. It laid them low. How will you stand? Believe it! Those that have been lions in peace have behaved like deer in this war. Brutus, who seemed to be as courageous as any, cried out like a child when Furius came to slit his throat. Heathen, who see nothing in death except rottenness and corruption, which look no farther than the grave, have esteemed death the king of terrors and the terrible of terrible. They have been frightened into a fever upon the sight of its forerunner. However, death is not half as terrible to a moral heathen as it will be to you, oh wicked Christian! You know that your day of death is your day of doom. You know that the axe of death will cut you down as fuel for the unquenchable fire. You know that as soon as you are carried from the earth, you are cast into hell. Yet you presume that you will behave like a man at the onslaught of this enemy. I dare to prophesy that your courage will be less than a child's. Man, do you not know, as Pilate said to Christ, that death has power to kill you as well as release you (John 19:10)? It can send your body to the grave and your soul to the place of endless misery.

5. Death Is a Misery

Fifth, do you realize that misery awaits every carnal man at death? In your lifetime, you do the devil's work. When death comes, he will pay you your wages. Sin, at present, is a bee with honey in its mouth, but, at death, the sting in its tail will appear. At present, you have your savory food and sugared drinks, but, at death, the reckoning comes. Some tell us that candy, although pleasant to the taste, is very heavy in the stomach. I am certain that the sweet morsels of sin, upon which you so merrily feed, will one day lie heavier than lead on your heart. They will be more bitter than gall and wormwood.

You may see now and then in this world, through the floodgates, some drops of wrath leaking out upon your soul. However, when death comes, the floodgates will be fully opened. Then, oh then, what a torrent of wrath will come pouring down upon you! Here, you sip the cup of the Lord's fury, but then you will drink the last drop. The pains, which you suffer here, are but an earnest of your eternal punishment. It was a cruel mercy, which Tamerlane showed to three hundred lepers, in killing them to rid them of their misery. Yet, death will be altogether merciless and cruel to you, for it only frees you from the jail to carry you to the gallows. It will deliver you from whips, but scourge you with scorpions. Its little finger will be infinitely heavier than anything experienced in this miserable life. When God says to death concerning you, as Judas to the Jews concerning Christ, "Take him and lead him away safely" (Mark 14:44), who knows the mocking, buffetings, piercings, scourging, plus the cursed, painful, shameful, and eternal death, that will follow?

Suppose, for your soul's sake, that you are climbing the stairs to your bedroom, from where you will never return until carried on men's shoulders. You look at your body, and see death's forerunner, sickness, preparing his way before him. Oh, how your color comes and goes at the sight of this axe, which the hand of death has laid at the root of your tree of life! Now you are lying on that bed from which you will never arise. Your chief concern is to look for some shelter against the approaching storm. You look upward and see God, full of fury, whom you dared so many times to the face by resolving that, since you would live without His counsels, you will die without His comforts. You look downward and see Satan, who at one time was your flatterer and apparent friend. Now, he is your tormentor and desperate foe, waiting, like the jailer, to drag you to his den. You look inward, and conscience presents to you a black catalogue of your bloody crimes. In the name of God, it arrests you for your sins, and charges you to answer for them at God's dreadful tribunal, to which you are going. You look outward, and see your friends, relations, and earthly comforts. You seek the living among the dead, but, alas, it is not there. Your wife, children, and neighbors may weep with you, but they cannot reduce your grief. On the contrary, they may actually give you cause to call to remembrance your sins. However, they cannot ease the least of your sorrows. They are miserable comforters, physicians of no value.

I have read of a woman, condemned for killing her child, who—while being dragged to her execution—looked pitifully at her father and mother: "Will you not help me? Where is your compassion? How can you allow your own child to be so cruelly treated?" However, they could not help her. Truly, such is your case! You look to your right and left, to your father, mother, husband, house, and land, and you call for help. Nevertheless, they cannot give you any comfort in this groaning hour, in this dreadful conflict. They may be near your body, as ravens about a carcass, to devour it (i.e., to get something from you), but they cannot defend it.

Now, the screech owl of death, which was clawing outside your window, has entered your room. It flies toward your bed. The messenger has come to show you the warrant for your speedy and immediate execution. Now, now, is the beginning of your sorrows! You cannot live, and you dare not die. You desire to be rid of your pain by death, yet you fear you will go to a worse place. You choose to stay, but death will not be denied. You must go! You say, "I am not ready; I have important earthly matters to finish. I am not prepared; I have the salvation of my soul, a work of infinite weight, to begin. So, I ask you to excuse me." You beg for one week, one day, one hour, but death will not wait one moment. Death pulls you towards the place of your eternal punishment. Your soul clings to your body like Joab to the altar, not wanting to let go (1 Kings. 2:28–34). However, death, like Solomon's soldier, rips you in pieces by force and slays you there.

Now your soul stands quivering upon your pale lips, ready to take its flight to its eternal home. You see devils, like so many ravening and roaring lions, looking and longing, for you—their prey. Your past sins trouble you. Oh, how you curse your pastimes and pleasures, your companions and possessions, which stole away your time and affections and hindered your preparation for such a dreadful hour! Your future sufferings terrify you.

Oh, you think to yourself, "Where am I going? Where will my soul dwell this night? In what place, with what persons, will I dwell forever? Oh, that I had prepared for this beforehand! How many times did God call me, ministers persuade me, Christ beseech me, and conscience warn me? Nevertheless, I was a fool! I rejected the entreaties of Christ, stifled the convictions of conscience, scorned the counsels of men, ignored the commands of God, and trampled on Sabbaths, sermons, and seasons of grace. I treated them as worthless things. Now, my day is past, my soul is lost, heaven's gate is shut. Woe, it is too late! The blessed God, in whose favor is life, to whom I said, 'Depart from me,' has now fixed my doom to depart from Him forever. Oh, what inconceivable evil is there in the loss of so great a good! Ten thousand hells are included in my banishment from that heaven. The frightful and cruel devils, whom I defied in my words, but deified in my heart and works, whose lusts were my laws, and whose wills were my warrant, will be my masters, tyrants, and tormentors for all eternity. My own soul (Oh that I could flee from myself!) is infinitely more grievous and painful than ever any sword was to flesh. What wolf in the breast, what pangs of the stone, what pain of the teeth, what cancer in the bowels, ever caused the slightest part of that torture, which the worm in my conscience causes! However, it is as impossible for me to avoid it as for the wounded deer to run from the arrow that sticks in its side. The fire burns me, yet consumes me not. It gives heat to scorch me, but no light to refresh me. Here is blackness of darkness, yet I can see the heart-cutting frowns of an angry God. I can see myself to be infinitely miserable. I enjoy a long night, but no rest. I must always complain, but have no relief. Here is crying without compassion, pain without pity, and sorrow without the smallest drop of comfort.

If my misery were to end at some point, even if it were after millions of ages, my heart would have some hope. However, alas, alas, as it is intolerable, so it is unchangeable! As long as God is God, I must fry in these flames. Not all my tears can quench the least spark of this fire. Although I weep forever, all this fire will not dry up the least tear. Oh, that I had never been! Oh, that I might never be! What! Must I live forever, and yet never live? Must I die forever, and yet never die? Consider this, all of you that pass by: Is there any sorrow like our sorrows, with which the Lord afflicts us in the day of His fierce wrath? Who can dwell in such everlasting burnings? Who can abide such devouring flames? Oh, that the mountains would fall on us, and the hills cover us, hiding us from the presence of Him who sits upon the throne and from the wrath of the Lamb, because the day of His wrath is come, and who can stand (Rev. 6:16–17)! Oh, what a dreadful sunset of life will it be that brings such a dismal night of eternal death!"

Oh, friend, think of this now: How will you die? If you leave this life in the service of your lusts, you are irrecoverably lost, and you are miserable beyond all expression and conception. If Job, because of some temporal calamity, cursed the day he was born and the messenger that announced his birth and desired to die rather than to endure it, who will you curse (Job 3:2–3)? Or rather, who will you not curse when under the sense of eternal misery? Surely, you will seek for death, but not find it; dig for it, but it will flee from you. Although Judas could have made a way out of the hell he had on earth, he cannot make a way out of the hell he has in hell. When you die, God Himself judges you. There is no appeal or reversing His judgment. "It is appointed unto men once to die, but after this the judgment" (Heb. 9:27).

6. You Must Prepare for Death

Sixth, do you realize that happiness would be yours at death, if you were prepared for it? As the good housewife expects winter without fearing it, being prepared with extra clothing, so you may expect death without fearing it, being prepared with proven armor. Although sinners roar bitterly when they behold that sea of scalding lead in which they must swim naked forever, you may, like the apostle, desire to depart (Phil. 1:23). You may wish for that hour when you will loose anchor and sail to Christ. It is possible for your dying day to be your wedding day, as the martyrs called it, for then the fairest of ten thousand and your soul will be solemnly knit together.

As terrifying as death is to others, you may—like a weary child—ask to be put to bed, knowing that it will send you to your everlasting happy rest. If it is a happy death to die willingly, you should give up the ghost and volunteer for that war. Nature teaches that death is the end of misery, but grace teaches you that death will be the beginning of your felicity. It cannot hurt you. It may destroy the body, but, when that is done, it has done all it can. It is like a fierce watchdog that has lost its teeth. It may bark and tear at your coat, but it cannot bite to the bone. This bee, death, fastened her sting in Christ's blessed body. Since then, it has been but a buzz in the ears of Christ's mystical body. Although the wicked are gathered at death (Ps. 26:9), as sticks for the fire, or as grapes for the winepress of God's wrath, you will be gathered (according to Isa. 57:2) as women gather flowers—to preserve them.

Death will exceedingly help you. You may, like Samson, fetch meat out of this eater and sweetness out of this strong lion (Judg. 14:14). Death, ever since it walked to mount Calvary, has turned (for believers) into the gate of life. A heathen could say, "Life is not taken away from me by the immortal gods, but death is given to me," meaning as an act of grace and favor. How much more may a Christian esteem death, for it puts an end to his trials, sins, and troubles. It is a privilege rather than a punishment. "Blessed are the dead which die in the Lord...that they may rest from their labors" (Rev. 14:13). When sickness first informs you that death is near, you may welcome the servant for bringing you the good news of his approaching master. Your heart may leap for joy to think that, although you are, like Peter (Acts 12:4–7), now bound in the chains of sin and imprisoned among sinners, the angel is coming who will with one blow on your side, cause your chains to fall off, open the prison doors, and release your soul into the glorious liberty of the sons of God.

When this Samuel comes to your gate, you need not, as the elders of Bethlehem, tremble at his coming (1 Sam. 16:45). If you ask the question, "Comest thou peaceably?" he will answer, "Yes, peaceably. I come to offer up a sacrifice of a sweet smelling savor, acceptable to God in Jesus Christ." The pale face of death will please you better than the greatest beauty on earth. When you lie on your dying bed, and physicians have given up hope, Christ will visit you and give your soul such a remedy that you may walk in the valley of the shadow of death and fear no evil. How willingly may you part with the militant members of Christ for the triumphant saints! How cheerfully may you leave your nearest relations for your dearest Father and Elder Brother! How comfortably may you leave all the riches, honors, and pleasures of this life, knowing that, although death comes to others in order to take away their fleshly comforts and carnal contentment (all their hopes, happiness, and heaven), yet it comes to you only as a servant.

When your soul is ready to bid your body "goodnight," until the morning of the resurrection, you may joyfully commit your body to the grave, as a bed of spices, and may see glorious angels waiting on your soul, carrying it, like Elijah (2 Kings. 2:11), in a triumphant chariot into heaven's blessed court. There the noble host and celestial choir of saints and angels will greet you and the holy Jesus and gracious God, in the fruition of whom you will be perfectly happy forever and ever, will welcome you. If there was so much rejoicing in heaven at your repentance (when you first set out on this journey), what joy will there be when, through so many hazards and hardships, you arrive at your journey's end!

Friend, if you were prepared, death would be to you a change from a prison to a palace, from sorrows to solace, from pain to pleasure, from heaviness to happiness. All your sins and sorrows would be buried in your grave, and the ship of your soul—which in this life is weather-beaten, tossed up and down with the boisterous waves of temptation and the high winds of the world's wrath and the devil's rage—would arrive at a blessed and everlasting harbor. Death would sound the retreat, and call you out of the battlefield—where the bullets fly thick in your combat with the flesh, world, and wicked one—to receive a crown of life. Hence, the ancient custom of placing a laurel crown at the head of the dead man's coffin in token of victory and triumph.

CHAPTER 7

How to Be Prepared to Die

If anything, or all, that I have written has led you to prepare yourself for your death, if these motives (which your conscience must acknowledge to be weighty) have melted you and made you ready for a divine stamp, then I will acquaint you with the means as to how you may die well. Having finished what is persuasive, I offer you that which is directive.

Know, reader, that there is no other medicine in the world that can cure your wounded, dying soul, but what I prescribe for you. If you throw it away, or neglect the rules for applying it to your wounds, then your lamentable condition will be irrecoverable and your dreadful state will be desperate. I will not try new inventions on your bleeding, gasping soul, but give you that remedy (consisting of only two ingredients) that the Great Physician has left in writing with His own hand. Thousands have found it to be effectual for their cure.

Pride, or an ambitious desire for self-sufficiency and self-subsistence, was the stone over which man first stumbled, thereby falling into the bottomless pit of matchless misery. The fatal knife cut the throat of his glorious hopes and happiness. In man's recovery, the wise God, like a tender father, takes special care to remove these dangers out of the children's way. For this reason, He has chosen two graces (which point the most to our beggarliness and carry us the most out of ourselves) to make us happy and lead us to Him: faith and repentance.

Faith teaches us to deny ourselves as utterly weak. Repentance causes us to abhor ourselves as altogether unworthy. Repentance reveals our nakedness and obnoxiousness, and thereby our shame and suffering. Faith tells us that our own rags come infinitely short of hiding our nakedness, and that we must fetch our garments out of someone else's wardrobe. The whole globe of Christianity divides itself into these two hemispheres: faith and repentance.

Therefore, reader, if you want to die well (i.e., undergo that great change with comfort), then it is absolutely and indispensably necessary that you pay attention to these two changes beforehand: (1) a change in your state or condition, which is brought about by faith; and (2) a change in your nature or disposition, which is brought about by repentance. The door of your happiness hangs on these two hinges: (1) the merit of Christ outside you, and its acceptance by God for the justification of your person; and (2) the Spirit of Christ within you, and His operation for the sanctification of your nature.

1. A Change in State by Faith

First, there must be a change in your state by faith in Christ, or else you can never enter the other world with comfort. There is no such shroud for the wrapping of your departed soul as the righteousness of a Savior. Paul's concern was that he might not be found naked (2 Cor. 5:3). Oh, it is sad indeed for your soul to be summoned to appear before the jealous God, and to have nothing to cover its nakedness! Adam, knowing that he was naked, fled from God (Gen. 3:8). Guilt cannot be anything but shy in the presence of the judge. Sore eyes will not endure the sight of the sun. God is a consuming fire to all those who do not have Jesus Christ as their screen. He says to every person, as Joseph to the patriarchs, "Ye shall not see my face, except your brother be with you" (Gen. 43:3). It is only in the garments of your elder brother, Christ, that you have hope of receiving the blessing. Everyone who dies outside of Christ, dies in his sins (John 8:21). Were not men's hearts so desperately hardened, it would be impossible for any to die in their senses that die in their sins! All would die demented who die thus defiled!

By nature, you are under the covenant of works, and therefore you are bound to earn happiness by your own effort. However, no mere man ever sailed to bliss in that ship! You are liable to the curse of the law. You are a bond slave to your jailer, Satan, and an heir of hell. If, therefore, you would ever arrive at heaven's blessed port, you must embark in a different ship—the covenant of grace, by which you may be set free from all the crosses and curses of the law, and be filled with all the special comforts and rich remedies of the gospel. Now, it is faith in Christ by which you enter this ship. Surely, then, it concerns you to get this grace! Many, if not millions, are drowned by sailing through the boisterous billows of death in the broken ship of the first covenant. However, others sail triumphantly to their desired haven in the covenant of grace.

Reader, if you are outside of this covenant, then you are like a man in the midst of the sea without a boat. You are sure to sink. It is said that a man, at the point of drowning in a river, saw a rainbow in the sky (the sign of God's covenant that He would never again drown the world), and made this conclusion: "If God saves the whole world from a deluge of waters yet suffers me to perish in this river, then what good will that covenant do me?" So I say to you: Although thousands escape a deluge of wrath through God's promise to Christ and in Christ to His purified ones, what good will it do you if you perish?

An interest in this covenant was the living comfort of dying David: "Although my house be not so with God; yet he hath made with me an everlasting covenant, ordered in all things, and sure: for this is all my salvation, and all my desire, although he make it not to grow" (2 Sam 23:5). It is important to note how the pious king draws all the wine that made his heart glad from this cask. Death is one of the sourest things in the world. Such things require much sugar to make them sweet. David found so much honey in the covenant that it turned death into a pleasant, desirable meal. If you look at the beginning of the chapter, you will find that his death was near: "Now these be the last words of David" (2 Sam. 23:1). However, his heart was at ease, because God's covenant was everlasting. Death is famous for its terror and its power. It tears down the mighty princes and potentates of the earth. Samson was but a child in death's hands. For this reason, when Scripture describes strength in its full proportion, it states, "as strong as death" (Song 8:6). However, as strong as death is, David knew it could not break asunder the covenant between God and him, nor dissolve the union between his Savior and his soul.

Faith finds a sure footing in the firmness of this covenant. Yes, God's covenant puts life into a dying Christian. Although death parted the soul and body of Christ, it was unable to part either of them from the divine nature. They were like a sword drawn by a man, in that the sword is in one hand, separated from the sheath in the other hand, but neither of them is separated from the man. Therefore, although death breaks the natural union between the believer's soul and body, it cannot break the mystical union between Jesus Christ and the soul. For this reason, saints are said to "sleep in Jesus" (1 Thess. 4:14).

Truly, by virtue of this covenant, they do not fly back at the sight of their foe (death), but look him in the face with courage and confidence. They triumph over him, as if he were already under their feet: "O death, where is thy sting? O grave, where is thy victory? The sting of death is sin; and the strength of sin is the law. But thanks be to God, which giveth us the victory through our Lord Jesus Christ" (1 Cor. 15:55–57). They speak as challengers, daring their disarmed enemy to meet them in the battlefield. They speak as conquerors, assured (through the captain of their salvation) of victory even before they fight. It is certain that, at Calvary, Christ accomplished something that made the Christian's bed soft and easy. It would have been a bed of thorns, but Christ turned it into a bed of feathers. Therefore, the believer lies down to sleep sweetly and comfortably.

By this time, reader, I hope you understand the necessity and benefit of this relative change. With this covenant, you are armed with the righteousness of Christ, which is law-proof, death-proof, and judgment-proof. This covenant leaves death wholly disarmed and naked. Without this, you have no weapons, and find death to be a man of war. You know that sin is the sting of death, and that the strength of sin is the law. The law binds the soul to its curse and punishment, because of the soul's disobedience. It already passes a sentence of condemnation upon the creature, and begins its execution in the bondage and fear (as flashes of the unquenchable fire) that men experience in this life (John 3:18; Rom. 7:6; Heb. 2:14). As sin derives its strength from the law (the law making it powerful enough to curse and condemn), so death derives its strength and sting (its venom and virtue), to kill, damn, and destroy soul and body forever, from sin.

Sin makes death so deadly. It is the poison in the cup that makes it so mortal and loathsome to drink. Your work and wisdom, therefore, is (as the Philistines, when they heard that the great strength of Samson, the destroyer of their country, lay in his hair) to cut it off (Judg. 16:19). You know where the strength of death (the great destroyer and damner of souls) lies. Therefore, you must be careful, night and day, to seek God with sighs and sobs, strong cries and deep groans, for pardon of sin. In addition, you must be careful to give yourself no rest until you attain an interest in this covenant through Jesus Christ.

Pious Job was exceedingly desirous for a sense of pardon: "And why dost thou not pardon my transgression, and take away mine iniquity? For now shall I sleep in the dust; and thou shalt seek me in the morning, but I shall not be" (Job 7:21). He cries out, as one who has fallen into a deep, dirty ditch, or one whose house is ablaze, "Water, water for the Lord's sake, to cleanse this defiled soul, and to quench this scorched conscience!" What is the reason behind his desire? Job was going to appear before his judge, and he dare not venture into

God's presence without a pardon in his hand. The child does not dare to go to bed at night until he has asked his father's blessing, and begged and obtained forgiveness for his disobedience during the day.

Nothing, in the whole creation can ease the conscience that is tormented with the guilt of sin and terrified with the fear of death. Only the blood of this covenant can bring such peace. A bandage, spread with the blood of Christ, and applied by faith to the sore, is a sovereign and certain cure. Faith in Christ is such a shield that under its protection a Christian may stand in the evil day of death, keep his ground, and guard himself from all the arrows that the law, Satan, and conscience can aim at him. "I am the resurrection, and the life: he that believeth in me, though he were dead, yet shall he live" (John 11:25).

The death of the King of saints is the only comfort and help against death, the king of terrors. Christ took man's disease and died, so that all who look on Him with an eye of faith may recover and live. The Red Sea of His blood is the only way through which you can enter Canaan. Reader, since there is a flood (vengeance and wrath) coming upon the world, fly, as the distressed dove (Gen. 3:8), to this ark of the covenant! Jesus Christ, the true Noah, a preacher of righteousness, puts forth His hand to take you to Himself. He is the Son of David, to whom souls that are in debt and in distress may flee. He speaks to you, as David to Abiathar, "Abide thou with me, fear not: for he (the world and devil) that seeketh my life seeketh thy life: but with me thou shalt be in safeguard" (1 Sam. 22:23).

2. A Change in Nature by Repentance

Second, there must be a change in your nature by repentance, or else death can never be your passage into the undefiled inheritance. The new man is the only citizen of the New Jerusalem. It is foolish to attempt a voyage to the "Happy Islands" in an old, leaking boat. In the art of navigation, it was a law (and formerly seriously observed) that no one could be a master or master's mate, who had not previously been an oarsman. No one is fit to reign with God, who has not produced for God.

Men must be apprentices on earth to that high and holy trade of worshipping and glorifying the blessed God, and know the art and mystery of it, before they can enrich themselves by it in heaven. Men, who are strangers to a country and unacquainted with its language and culture, find it to be a lonely place. He, whose eyes are so bad that he cannot see God with the help of the spectacles of ordinances, is also unable to see Him face to face. Alas, what would an earthly man do in heaven?

Until you are converted, possessing a sense of your sins and miseries, you are a rebel in arms against God. If death finds you in such a condition, if God takes the fort of your soul by storm while your weapons are in your hands, then you can expect nothing less than eternal death without mercy. There is no peace with God while you wage war against Him. The sinner, instead of disarming, arms death against himself. The life of sin is the life of death, in that it enables death to kill the soul. Until your nature is renewed, your heart is full of enmity against God, and your life is nothing but rebellion against Him. As a result, you can have no delight or joy in Him, who is the very heaven of heavens.

There must be conformity to God before there can be communion with Him. God and man must agree before they can walk or dwell together. "Except ye be converted, ye can in no wise enter into the kingdom of God" (Matt. 18:3). "Except a man be born again, he cannot see the kingdom of God" (John 3:3). These negative expressions—*"can in no wise enter"* and *"cannot see"*—point to the impossibility of it on God's part, because He is fully set against it, and to the incapacity of it on man's part, because he is wholly unprepared for it. Swine are not fit for a furnished room. As timber must be dried and shrunk before it is fit for building, otherwise it will warp, so God must humble and draw out self-sap before people become the temple of the Holy Ghost. The building that reaches to heaven must have a deep foundation.

Those who attempt to turn pewter by alchemy into silver must first dissolve the pewter. If not, their labor is in vain. Likewise, your heart must be melted by godly sorrow for sin and hatred of sin before you can be a vessel of silver, fit for your Master's use. The angel stirred the waters before the sick were healed (John 5:4). "Repent...that your sins may be blotted out" (Acts 3:19). Repentance and remission are eternal twins. It is observable that nature has made the fruit of many trees, whose roots are bitter, to be very sweet. Those who sow tears in life, reap joy at death. The wet seedtime enjoys the sunny harvest. God is resolved that all the sons of men will feel their sin, either in broken bones on earth or broken backs in hell.

When sin receives its death wound before death, it will expire at death, for although sin brought death into the body, death will cast sin out of the body. When grace buds and blossoms before death, it will ripen into glory at death. Holiness is the raiment of needlework, in which you will be brought to your Lord and husband (Ps. 45:14). However, it is necessary that, like Abraham's ram (Gen. 22:13), you are troubled in the briars before you are offered up by death as a peace offering to God. Those who dream of being carried to heaven in a feather bed are foolish. Only those who are weary of the work (as a sick man of his bed) and heavy laden with the weight of sin (as a porter of his burden) will enter into everlasting rest.

Naturalists observe that, when the Egyptian fig tree is put into water, it immediately sinks to the bottom. However, when it is well soaked, contrary to the nature of other trees, it floats to the top. Until your mind is enlightened to see sin's deformity, your will is renewed to refuse sin as your only enemy, and your affections are purified to grieve for sin and hate it as contrary to the blessed God and your own happiness, until your soul is soaked in these bitter waters, you can never expect to be lifted up to the rivers of pleasures at God's right hand. This howling wilderness is the only way to Canaan. The path to Zion lies by Sinai. God only pours the oil of gladness into the broken vessel. Some philosophers tell us that feeling is the foundation of natural life—if there is no feeling, then there is no life. I am sure it is true in divinity. If there is no feeling and sense of sin, then there is no spiritual and eternal life. A lack of feeling is deadly and damning.

God qualifies all those whom He intends to dignify. Saul is qualified to reign over men by receiving a different spirit than he had before (1 Sam. 11:6). How much more must those, who will reign with God, be qualified by receiving a new heart and a new spirit! The sun never leaps from midnight to midday; first, it sends forth some glimmerings of light in the dawning of the day; then, it sends forth some weak beams of light; then, it shines upon us with open face as it runs to its meridian glory. Similarly, God never carries a soul from hell to heaven, from the natural condition to the blissful vision, but through the door or gate of conversion.

Reader, to conclude this use and summarize these two particulars, which are worth more than the whole world, I will draw a little closer to you, so that you may see how willing I am to be instrumental in your welfare.

Oh, that I knew what savory spiritual meat you love most! If possible, I would set it before you, so that you may eat and your soul might bless God before you die. For your eternal good, I have a special gift to offer you from the blessed God: marriage to His only Son, the Lord Jesus Christ. This day, I am sent to you, as His ambassador, with full instructions to woo you on His behalf, so that I may present you to Christ as a chaste virgin. You do not need to doubt my authority, for you may find my commission in the Scriptures. You do not need to question God's sincerity in His offer, notwithstanding all your unworthiness, for He sent His Son on a great journey from heaven to earth to marry your nature, so that He may be married to your person. At infinite cost, He has provided glorious attire and precious jewels out of heaven's wardrobe and cabinet, so that you may be adorned in a manner that is fit for the spouse of so great a Lord. He has sent you His Son's picture, which is of greater value than heaven and earth. It is found in the gospel, where He is drawn in all His royalty, beauty, and glory.

Friend, look at Him, and consider His person, for He is fairer than the children of men are. He is the express image of His Father's person. Your beloved (oh, shall I call Him so!) is white and ruddy, the fairest of ten thousand (Song 5:10). He is altogether lovely (Song 5:16). He is nothing but loveliness! No one has ever seen Him without being enamored with Him.

Look at His portion: He is heir of all things. All power is given to Him in heaven and earth. I know your poverty, but there are unsearchable riches in Christ, even durable riches and righteousness. You are infinitely in debt, and thereby liable to the arrest of divine justice and eternal imprisonment in hell. However, I tell you that the riches of this emperor are able to discharge the debts of millions of worlds, and to leave enough left over for their comfortable and honorable living for all eternity.

Look at His parentage: He is the only begotten of the Father, full of grace and truth, the eternal Son of God. As there is incomparable beauty and favor in His person, and inestimable riches and treasure in His portion, so there is inconceivable dignity and honor in His parentage. He is the only natural Son and heir of the most high God. For your further encouragement, He is your near kinsman, bone of your bone and flesh of your flesh. Therefore, He has a right to you. God has commanded His stewards, as Abraham his servant (Gen. 24:4–5) not to take a wife for His son from among the daughters of the Canaanites or from among the evil angels, but to go to His Son's country and kindred, and to take a wife for Him from among the children of men.

Friend, you are aware of the errand for which I am sent to you. I hope there is an arrow of love aimed at you from the gracious eyes of this Lord of glory, so that you are wounded at heart, taken with Him, and led to cry, "Oh, that I would have the honor and happiness of becoming the bride of so lovely a bridegroom! Oh, that this King of saints would take me, a poor sinner, into His bed and bosom!" I hope you can say, as Abigail when David sent to take her as his wife, "Behold, let thine handmaid be a servant to wash the feet of the servants of my lord" (1 Sam. 25:41).

If it is like this with you, it means that your affections are already captivated. For your comfort, you should know that He is not like those, who, when they have gained another's goodwill, cast him away. However, it is necessary that you understand what He requires of you, in order to avoid any future surprises. Plain dealing is extremely important in marriage. Those who have entered marriage in haste have found cause to repent at leisure. Therefore, I will propound two arguments for your encouragement, and then demand your agreement to two articles, upon which this marriage must be established.

3. Two Arguments

The first argument is this: Consider the necessity of accepting Christ as your husband. It is impossible to obtain heaven as your inheritance without marrying the One who is the heir. It may be that, as the man who was unwilling to marry Ruth (Ruth 4:2–4), you are ready for the portion, but unwilling to marry the person. You are anxious to be pardoned, adopted, and saved, but unwilling to take Jesus Christ for your husband lest you lose your sinful pleasures, and thereby mar (in your opinion) a better inheritance. However, know this: the day you buy the field, you must marry the owner. The day you gain the invaluable privileges of the gospel, you must marry Christ—the purchaser and owner of those privileges.

It is impossible to obtain the precious fruit without owning the tree that bears it. Indeed, your marriage to Christ is so fruitful that you do not need anything else. It includes forgiveness of sins, the love of God, peace of conscience, joy in the Holy Ghost, eternal life, every good thing, and all good things. You cannot even imagine what a numerous posterity of Barnabases (i.e., sons of consolation) would result from such a wedding! However, without this blessing, you are completely and eternally lost. Beware, oh beware, if you refuse such an offer! You must marry Christ, or be damned forever!

The second argument is this: Consider God's mercy and humility in offering you such a fortune! Earthly kings will not stoop so low (unless forced) as to match their only sons with their subjects. When their sons marry, they do so with the highest families—those that sparkle most with the diamonds of birth, beauty, riches, and glory. Hear, oh heavens; be astonished, oh earth; wonder, oh reader, at this low stoop of the infinite God! He is willing, even earnest, that His only Son and heir, the King of kings, should marry His creature. There is an infinite distance and disproportion between them. The Son does not wed His noblest creatures: the angels. He weds men—sinful, polluted dust and ashes.

That our spiritual souls should be joined to our earthly bodies is a great wonder. However, that God should marry man is infinitely greater! It is said of the king of Babylon that he removed Jehoiachin from prison, spoke kindly to him, removed his prison garments, and set his throne above the thrones of the other kings in his presence (2 Kings 25:27–29). Man was a poor prisoner, chained with his own corruptions, guarded by the devil, and condemned to suffer the pains of eternal death. Oh the loving-kindness of God! He sends His only Son to open the prison doors, having first satisfied the law and removed its curse, which was like a padlock on the prison gate to keep it closed. He sets the poor captives at liberty, changes their nasty prison garments, and exalts their nature above the nature of glorious angels by marrying it to Himself. Can you find it in your heart, friend, to abuse such matchless grace and favor? Is not the beggar mad, who refuses the offer of marriage from a gracious emperor? Will majesty stoop to misery in vain? It is supreme humility on God's side to make such an offer to you. It is the highest preferment of which you are capable—to such an extent, that it would have been blasphemy to desire it, if God had not offered it!

4. Two Articles

I come now to the articles of this marriage. Truly, they are nothing more than what you require of your own wife (if you have one). Therefore, you must acknowledge that they are reasonable. I will put them before you in two questions.

The first is this: Are you heartily willing to take Jesus Christ for your Savior and Sovereign? Can you love Him with a superlative love as your husband? It is one thing to love a man as a friend, and it is another thing to love him as your husband. Can you give Him the keys of your heart, and keep your affections as a fountain sealed up from others and open only for Him and in subordination to Him? Will you honor Him with the highest honor as your Lord, submitting to His Spirit as your guide and to His law as your rule? Is your soul so ravished with the beauty of His person, the excellency of His promises, and the equity of His precepts, that you dare to promise, through His strength, to be a loving, faithful, and obedient wife? Have the hot beams of that love, which shine forth from this Sun of righteousness as the rays of the sun united in a glass, turned you into a flame, so that your heart is now ascending and mounting to heaven where your beloved is? Can you no more live without Him than your body live without your soul? Are you willing to be sanctified by His Spirit, so that you may be prepared for His embrace? Are you willing to be saved by His merits alone, as the only procuring cause of all your hopes and happiness? Will you take Him for better and for worse, for richer and for poorer, with His cup of affliction as well as His cup of consolation, with His shameful cross as well as His glorious crown? Will you choose to suffer with Him rather than reign without Him, to die for Him rather than live without Him? As you know, those who marry must expect trouble in the flesh. Christianity always draws clouds and afflictions after it, but your future glory and pleasure will reward you abundantly for your present pain and humiliation.

The second question is this: Will you divorce your other lovers, and guard the bed of your heart for Him? Will the evil of sin continue to receive glances from you? As Amnon treated Tamar (2 Sam. 13:1–15), will the hatred with which you hate your filthy sins, with which you have committed spiritual fornication, be greater than the love with which you loved them? Can you send away the bondwoman and her son (Gen. 21:10), without it being sorrowful in your sight, so that your whole delight is in, and your entire estate is preserved for, the true Isaac? Will the Sun reign in the heavens of your heart without any competitor? When Rome established a dictator, all other authority ended. Likewise, if Christ is exalted in your soul, there must be an end of all other rule and power. Christ will not be mocked. Nor will He be like a stump of wood to frogs—something that lust can dance all over.

This marriage, so honorable and profitable, is offered to you upon these terms. If you agree to these two articles, you are secure forever. However, if you refuse, you are miserable above all comprehension for all eternity. What do you say? Will I ask you the same question that they asked Rebekah, "Wilt thou go with this man?" (Gen. 24:58). A negative response is nothing less than eternal death.

In your acceptance of the offer, there is nothing less than heaven and eternal life. What would you be willing to do to continue your natural life? What then should you be willing to do or suffer for eternal life? Perhaps you desire some time to consider the offer. Perhaps you are as Rebekah's mother—in favor of the match, but desirous to delay the wedding (Gen. 24:55). Augustine bewails this very thing in himself. While God was drawing him to Christ, his carnal pleasures presented themselves before his eyes, declaring, "What! Will you leave us forever, and will we be no more with you forever?" He then threw himself to the ground, weeping, and crying out, "O Lord, how long, how long shall I say tomorrow? Why not today, Lord? Why not today? Why should there not be an end of my sinful life this hour?" Believe it: delays are dangerous, especially in matters of such importance!

If you answer with Rebekah, "I will go," then cheer up, poor soul! Whatever your life has been like, your husband is able and willing to pay all your debts. Come forth; behold your beloved in all His embroidery and glory. His arms are stretched out to embrace you. His lips are ready to kiss you. Oh, what a loving look He gives you! I am certain that you have a greater place in His heart than you have in your own. You do not think enough about the rings and robes, the dainties and delicacies, the grace, mercy, and peace, that He provides upon your return—a wandering prodigal (Luke 15:22–23). You do not need to turn to the world any longer for its coarse, carnal food. Your beloved will entertain you with precious and costly feasts at His own table. You will have bread to eat, which the world knows nothing about. If dangers and evils pursue you, you have your city of refuge at hand, where you are secure from the fear and fury of men and devils.

If you accept this offer, it will be life for you to think of death. You will lift up your head with joy when the day of your redemption draws near. Death will release you from both sin and sorrow. Your soul will be at liberty. You have taken in your full cargo for heaven, and therefore you may call (like a merchant that has all his goods on board the ship) to the captain to hoist up sail and set course for your everlasting harbor. Oh, how your heart will revive, with old Jacob's (Gen. 45:27), to see those wagons that are sent to take you to your dear Jesus! You know that He is Lord of the country and that He is able to make you feel welcome when you arrive.

At present, you are in the body, and therefore absent from the Lord. However, at that time, you will be forever with the Lord. If you refuse so great and so good an offer, choosing slavery to the flesh over this Christian liberty, and if you resolve (as many wicked people do) to choose many harlots rather than one wife, to love and serve various lusts and pleasures rather than marrying Jesus Christ, then be confident that your fleshly life (although pleasant at present) will soon cause troublesome sleep and frightful dreams. If you intend to launch into the ocean of eternity without this captain, the blessed Savior, who alone can steer the vessel of your soul in the midst of dangerous reefs and sands, and if you intend to disregard the passage you take and the port you arrive at in the other world, whether heaven or hell, then prepare yourself to take up your eternal lodging among frightening devils and to bear your part in the endless yelling and howling of the damned! Understand, to your terror, that this very offer of grace will one day, like Joab's sword to Abner (2 Sam. 3:27), stab you under the fifth rib, cut you to the very heart, and, like a mountain of lead, sink you deep into that ocean of wrath. There you will have plenty of time to condemn yourself for refusing so good an offer. In addition, there you will be tormented day and night forever.

"I call heaven and earth to record this day against you, that I have set before you life and death, blessing and cursing: therefore choose life, that both thou and thy seed may live: that thou mayest love the LORD thy God, and that thou mayest obey his voice, and that thou mayest cleave unto him: for he is thy life, and the length of thy days" (Deut. 30:19–20).

CHAPTER 8

Seek to Die Well

I will now speak to the serious Christian. If man's flesh will fail him, then you ought to fortify your soul, so that you are able to bid the flesh a cheerful farewell. Your care must be to die with courage. A good soldier, in all his armor, may be daunted at the sight of an enemy who appears without warning. Mary was troubled at the sight of the angel, who brought her the best news that ever the world has heard (Luke 1:30). It is true that you can never die before you are ripe for heaven, but you may die, in some sense, before you are ready in your own estimation to leave the earth. Many go to heaven certainly, who do not go to heaven comfortably.

According to Tertullian, the Christians in his time were "a sort of people prepared for death." When a son has loitered in the day, he is afraid to look his father in the face at night. However, when he has labored faithfully, he may enter his father's presence without fear. Although a man who is sober at home is better prepared to go to sleep at night than a man who is drinking and vomiting in a tavern, even so he may think of some business, neglected during the day, that makes him unable to go to sleep. Surely, this is part of the reason why many of the children of God are so agitated when the night of death approaches, and therefore go wrangling to bed.

Christian, in a few words, I want to direct you as to how you may put off your earthly tabernacle as cheerfully as your clothes, and lie down in your grave as comfortably as you do in your bed. It is your own fault if you do not maintain a good fire all day (I mean grace, enflaming the hearth of your heart), and therefore are unable to increase it at night so that you go to bed warm—to your eternal rest.

1. The First Means

You must be careful not to blot out your evidences for heaven. As you know, darkness is very dreadful. When men blur (by willful sins) the deeds that bespeak their right to heaven, so that they cannot read them, it is no wonder that they are afraid to leave the earth. It is reported of good Agathon that, when death approached, he was greatly troubled. His friends asked him, "What do you fear?" He answered, "I have endeavored to keep the commandments of God, but I am a man. How do I know whether my works please God or not?"

The man who does not know that he will go to a better place, will necessarily be troubled by the prospect of being removed from present pleasures. It is only assurance of a better life that will carry the soul with comfort through the bitter pangs of death. It was for this reason that Job called so frequently and cried so earnestly to be laid to bed: "Oh that I might have my request; and that God would grant me the thing that I long for! Even that it would please God to destroy me, that he would let loose his hand, and cut me off! Then should I yet have comfort; yea, I would harden myself in sorrow: let him not spare; for I have not concealed the words of the Holy One" (Job 6:8–10). Job had lived with a good conscience, and therefore he did not fear to die. His fidelity to God encouraged him to expect mercy from God. He had not concealed God's faithfulness from men, and therefore he knew that God would not conceal His loving-kindness from him.

David, on the other hand, when night drew near in his thoughts, was eager to live longer. God seemed to be calling him to bed (i.e., death), but David pleads, "O spare me, that I may recover strength, before I go hence, and be no more" (Ps. 39:13). Now, take note of the reason behind David's petition. As is generally accepted, Absalom was persecuting David at this time. The unnatural son forced his father to flee. In the cause of his suffering, David sees his own sin and God's indignation. He dreads to appear in the other world in such a condition. When things were clear between God and his soul, David could walk in the valley of the shadow of death and fear no ill—he could challenge death! However, now, when things are cloudy and dubious, David turns back like a coward. He has lost the sense of God's favor, and therefore he cannot think of venturing into God's presence without much fear. The train of his corruptions threatens to follow him to the highest court. He dare not appear before the Lord with such company. He has been declining in his grace under a sad disease of heart. As a weak, sickly man, he is afraid to travel so great a journey lest he should never return.

Friend, if you want to leave the world cheerfully, then live in the world conscientiously. Take heed of those fiends that will frighten you in the night of death. Choose suffering before sin. Punish your body to keep your soul pure. Some say that the mouse of Armenia would rather be taken and slain than preserved and polluted in a filthy hole. As the white is always in the archer's eye, so let your death always be in your eye in order that it may quicken you to diligence and exactness in life.

Logicians, who regard not the premises, arrive at wild conclusions. Likewise, if you are careless in your conduct, then you should expect an uncomfortable death. When God looked upon all His works, He saw that they were good. His Sabbath rest followed. Similarly, when you can reflect upon the various passages of your life, and see that, through Christ, they are good, and that you have not been guilty of enormities but of infirmities, then you can joyfully enter into your everlasting Sabbath. If conscience is kept clean, then your evidence will be clear. However, the truth is that many, even Christians, wound their souls by venturing into sin. As a result, they flinch and step back when it is time to be searched. In addition, they neglect to deal with their accounts for so long that they no longer know whether they are worth anything. Hence, they are unwilling to have their estates examined.

If you should fall, take heed of lying there. Be as speedy as possible in calling to Christ to raise you up! If your conscience is raw with the guilt of sin, then a light affliction (much more death) will make you kick, unwilling to bear it. However, when your flesh is sound (your soul healed by the blood of Christ), death itself will only be a light burden on your back. When you are sure of Christ's company, how happily may you (although you do not even have a penny in your wallet) go the way of all the earth and travel into the other world. He will bear your charges all the way.

2. The Second Means

Second, mortify your affections for the world and all its comforts. Those who love the world most, leave it worst. Lot's wife lingered in Sodom, and was unwilling to depart, because she loved it too much (Gen. 19:26). When boards merely lie upon one another, they are easy to separate. However, when they are glued to one another, it is impossible to separate them without tremendous effort. If your heart is loosely tied to the world, then it will be a small matter for you to leave it. However, if your affections are fastened to the world, then you will not leave it without much resistance and opposition.

The wife, who has kept her heart entirely for her husband, is always ready to open the door to him. However, she who entertains other lovers, dares not run to open the door when her husband knocks. First, she hurries to get her lovers out of sight. The more your affections are set on Christ, your true husband, the more the world is taken out of you, and therefore the easier it will be to take you out of the world. He who has laid up his heart in heaven, will think comfortably of laying down his head on earth. When the pins of the watch (which hold it together) are removed, how easily it falls to pieces. When your affections for the world are removed, how quickly and how quietly will your soul and body separate! If the world is as loose to you as your cloak, then you can take it off whenever you like. However, if it is as close to you as your skin, then those who try to persuade you to part with it will have an extremely difficult time. We read of some who were unwilling to die, because they had treasure in the field (Jer. 41:8). Where their treasure was, their hearts were also.

Make it your work, therefore, by considering the world's vanity and deceitfulness, and by pondering heaven's glory and happiness, to wean your heart from earthly things! If you do, you will willingly leave them as the infant leaves those breasts from which he was weaned long ago.

3. The Third Means

Third, accustom your heart to frequent thoughts of death. When children are frightened of a dog or a cat, we do not give way to their foolish fears. We bring the animal to them, get them to touch and handle it, and show them that it is not as frightening as they imagine. In time, they get over their fears, and even begin to play with it. Do you dread the king of terrors, death? Do not give way to this fear, but bring death up to your soul. Handle it and feel it. There is not as much pain in it as you imagine. There is nothing that should terrify you. In so doing, you will learn to play near the hole of this viper.

I suppose one reason why Job was not afraid of dying was his familiarity with death. Strangers are startled by things that are nothing to those who are accustomed to them. "I have said to corruption, Thou art my father: To the worm, Thou art my mother and my sister" (Job 17:14). Job was as familiar with death as with his father. He made no more of dying than of falling into the arms and embraces of his mother or sister. At first, Moses stepped back at the sight of the serpent (Ex. 4:3). However, when he had handled it a little, and it turned into a rod, it was no longer frightening to him.

There is a story of a donkey that terrified its master by running around in a lion's skin. Finally, the master figured it out. Having stripped off the lion's skin, he put the donkey to work for him. Perhaps you are afraid of this beast, death, supposing it to be a roaring lion.

However, if you get close, you will discover a donkey in a lion's skin. You will discover that it cannot hurt you, but can serve you in many ways. What is the death that frightens you? Is it not that which presents your faithful soul to your beloved Husband? Is it not that which enables you to leave the world and go to your Father? Is it anything less than a kiss from God's lips? When the baby is asleep, the indulgent parent will take him into her arms, and with many kisses lay him in her lap. The Chaldee paraphrase tells us that Moses died with a kiss of the Lord's mouth (Deut. 34:5).

Will it not be the funeral for all your corruptions and crosses? Will it not be the resurrection of all imaginable delights and comforts? Did you but know this, friend, you would not be so shy of its company. The Romans accustomed their youths to gladiator fights and bloody spectacles in order to make them less troubled by war. Before his death, Philostrates lived for seven years in his tomb, in order that his bones might be better known to his grave. You must accustom yourself to the thoughts of death—your change, your translation to bliss, and your entrance into heaven. When it comes, you will welcome it, knowing its errand so well. Mithridates accustomed his body to poison, and therefore turned it into good nourishment. Accustom your soul to the thoughts of death and, although it will be worse than poison to others, it will be pleasant and profitable to you!

CHAPTER 9

God Is Man's True Happiness

I now proceed to the second doctrine: the saint's comfort. It is taken from the second part of the text: "But God is the strength of my heart, and my portion forever" (Ps. 73:26). The comfort of a Christian in his saddest condition is this: God is his portion. The psalmist's condition was very sad: his flesh failed him. Man's soul often decays with his body. The two are let out together. The psalmist's heart fell with his flesh. But what was the strong medicine that kept him from fainting at such a season? Truly, it was this: "But God is the strength of my heart, and my portion for ever" (Ps. 73:26).

In winter, the sap retreats to the root of the tree, in order to be preserved. Likewise, in crosses such as death, the saint retreats to God, the fountain of his life, to be comforted. When his wives were captured, his wealth plundered, and his life threatened (for the soldiers talked of stoning him), David was in a dreadful state. One might think that such a heavy burden would break his back. However, the joy of the Lord was his strength!

"David encouraged himself in the Lord his God" (1 Sam. 30:6). When the table of earthly comforts (which had been spread so generously before him) was empty, David fetched sweetmeats out of his heavenly closet. He encouraged his heart in the Lord his God.

Christians, like the salamander, may live in the greatest fire of affliction. They may sing when the whole world is in a flame at the last day. The Spirit of God compares them to palm trees (Ps. 92:12), which (according to some naturalists) are never weighed down or dried up even though many weights are placed at the top of them and much drought is experienced at the bottom.

The only reason I will give for this doctrine is as follows: a godly man places his happiness in God. All things have a propensity (or inclination) towards that in which they place their felicity. A suitable and unchangeable rest is the only satisfaction of the rational creature. All the agitations of the soul are wings to carry man here and there, so that he may find a place to rest. When the eagle discovers and fastens on a carcass, it is content. The needle, pointing to the north, is quiet, although formerly it was in motion. In one place, the philosopher tells us that delight consists in motion, but elsewhere he tells us that it actually consists in rest.

Happiness is nothing but the Sabbath of our thoughts and the satisfaction of our hearts in the fruition of the chiefest good. The excellence of the object that we embrace in our hearts determines the degree of our happiness. The saint's choice is right—God alone is the soul's center and rest. Let a sinner have what he regards as his treasure and, although he is under many troubles, he is content. Give a covetous man wealth, and he will say, as Esau, "I have enough" (Gen. 33:9). When an ambitious man mounts up to a chair of state, he sits down at ease. If a lustful person can bathe himself in the streams of carnal pleasures, he is as a fish in his element. So, let a godly man enjoy his God, in whom he places all his joy and delight, in whom is all his happiness and heaven, he is well. He has all. "Shew us the Father, and it sufficeth us" (John 14:8). No more is desired.

No man thinks he is miserable until he has lost his happiness. A godly man is blessed when afflicted and buffeted, because he still has his God (Job 5:17). When a few leaves blow off, his comfort is that he still has the tree and its fruit. Like a man who is worth millions, he can rejoice even though he loses a few dollars. There is mention of a lake in the Salentine country called *Brimful*. You can put in what you like; it never runs over. You can draw out what you can; it never runs low. Such is the condition of a Christian. He never has too much. Moreover, take away what you will; he is still full, because he has God. Augustine affirms that there are two-hundred and eighty-eight opinions about happiness, but the philosophers were vain in their imaginations. I will clearly prove that the strength of man's happiness flows from an entirely different spring.

CHAPTER 10

God Alone Is Sufficient
for Man's Soul

There are things in God that make Him the saint's happiness and chief good. First, He is the saint's happiness because of His perfection and all-sufficiency. That which makes man happy must not have any want or weakness in it. It must be able to protect him against all evil and provide him with all good. The injuries of nature must be resisted and the shortcomings of nature must be supplied. This Sun of righteousness—like the great luminary of the world when it rises above the horizon—clears the air of mists and fogs and cheers the inhabitants with His light and heat. According to the degree of our enjoyment of Him, such is the degree of our happiness, or such is the degree of our freedom from evil and fruition of good.

Those who enjoy God perfectly in heaven know no evil. They are above all storms and tempests. They enjoy all good. "In his presence is fullness of joy" (Ps. 16:11). They have a perpetual spring and a constant summer, never understanding what an autumn or winter means.

The Christian, who enjoys God but imperfectly on earth, enjoys the same privileges but in part. His life is a mixture of day and night, light and darkness, good and evil. Evil cannot hurt him, but it may frighten him. He may taste the chief good, but his full meal is reserved until he enters his Father's house.

1. God Is Able to Free a Man from All Evil

The Greeks refer to a happy man as one who is not subject to death and misery. That which is man's happiness must be able, by its power, to protect him against all such perils. Creatures cannot provide this help, and therefore they cannot be our happiness. The man who trusts in second causes is like the one who, climbing to the top of a tree, sets his feet on rotten branches that will certainly break under his weight. Again, he is like the passenger who, in stormy weather, runs to some tottering outhouse that falls down on his head. However, God is the almighty guard.

The schoolmen tell us that the reason why Adam did not feel any cold in his state of innocence, even though he was naked, was his communion with God. God is the saint's shield to protect his body from all blows (Gen. 15:1). Therefore, He is compared in Scripture to those things and persons that shelter men in storms and defend men in dangers. At times, He is compared to a wall of fire, protecting travelers from wild beasts in the wilderness (Zech. 2:5). At times, He is compared to a wide river of water, defending a city against its enemies (Isa. 33:21). A good sentinel is very helpful for keeping a garrison safe. Therefore, God is said to watch and guard, "I the LORD do keep it…Lest any hurt it, I will keep it night and day" (Isa. 27:3). Although others are liable to nod and sleep when on guard, thereby giving the enemy an advantage, "He that keepeth Israel shall neither slumber nor sleep" (Ps. 121:4). He is so far from sleeping that He never slumbers. Some naturalists tell us that lions are insomniacs, possibly because their eyelids are too narrow for their eyes, and so they sleep with their eyes partly open. However, it is most true of the Lion of the tribe of Judah—He wakes, so that His people may sleep in safety. He is compared to a refuge: "Thou art my refuge and my portion" (Ps. 142:5). This is a metaphor for a fortress or castle, to which soldiers retreat for safety when beaten back by an overpowering enemy. Moreover, He is called "the LORD of hosts" (or, the general of His people), because, like a faithful commander, He is the first to enter, and the last to leave, the battlefield. God looks danger in the face before His people, and He makes certain they are safely out of the battlefield before He departs, "The LORD will go before you, and the God of Israel will be your rereward" (Isa. 52:12).

Travelers tell us that, from the top of the Alps, they can see great showers of rain below them while not one drop falls on them. Those who have God for their portion are in a high tower, and therefore they are safe from all troubles and showers. Not all the garments in this world can keep those who travel in downpours from being soaked to the skin. No creature is able to bear the weight of its fellow-creature. The creature is like a reed that breaks under the slightest weight. Again, the creature is like a thorn that pricks those who lean upon it. The bow drawn beyond its capacity breaks apart, and the string wound above its strength snaps in pieces. Such are all outward helps to those who trust in them in the midst of hardships.

However, Christians, anchored on the Rock of Ages, are secure in the greatest storm. They are like Zion, which cannot be moved. "In the time of trouble he shall hide me in his pavilion: In the secret of his tabernacle shall he hide me; he shall set me up upon a rock" (Ps. 27:5). God's sanctuary is His hiding place (Ezek. 7:22), and His saints are His hidden ones (Ps. 83:3). He hides them in His sanctuary from whatever may hurt them. For this reason, when it is stormy, He calls His children to come indoors out of the rain: "Come, my people, enter thou into thy chambers, and shut thy doors about thee; hide thyself as it were for a little moment, until the indignation be overpast" (Isa. 26:20).

The Christian, therefore, is encouraged in the face of evil, because God is his guard. He knows that, while he has this shield, he is bulletproof. "He shall cover thee with his feathers, and under his wings shalt thou trust" (Ps. 91:4). As the hen secures her young from the hawk and other ravenous birds by sheltering them under her wings, so God undertakes to protect His people. Through His strength they can triumph over trials and defy the greatest dangers. "At destruction and famine thou shalt laugh" (Job 5:22). They can also triumph over the greatest crosses, because they are more than conquerors through Him (Rom. 8:37).

2. God Is Able to Fill a Man with All Good

That which beautifies the rational creature must remove whatever is destructive and restore whatever is perfective. Weak nature must be supported, and empty nature must be supplied. Now, the whole creation cannot be man's happiness, because it is unable to defend him from evil and unable to delight him with good. The comfort that arises from creatures is like the juice of some plums—it fills with wind, but yields no nourishment. He who sits at the world's table, when it is largely spread and fairly furnished, and feeds most heartily upon its delights, is like the one who dreams he eats yet is hungry when he awakes. The best noise of earthly musicians makes but an empty sound; it may please the senses a little, but it cannot satisfy the soul in the least. The world has little to offer, and therefore produces but little cheer. Like a sick and queasy stomach, the very thing we desired so earnestly immediately sickens us. It was for this reason that those who esteemed their happiness to consist in pleasing their brutish part, vehemently desired new carnal delights. Nero had an officer who was called "an inventor of new pleasures." Suetonius observes the same of Tiberius, as does Cicero of Xerxes. These men, like children, quickly grew tired of that for which they were previously so desirous. The moralist (Seneca) gives us the reason for this: error is infinite. The thirst of nature may be satisfied, but the thirst of a disease cannot. The happiness of the soul consists in the enjoyment of that good which is equal to its desires. No creature, not all the creatures, is that good!

However, God is man's happiness, because He can satisfy him. The Hebrews describe a blessed man in the plural number, "blessednesses" (Ps. 32:1), because no man can be blessed with a single good, unless he abound in all good.

The soul of man is a vessel too large to be filled up with a few drops of water. However, God, who is an ocean, can fill it. Whatever is required to perfect deficient nature is found in God. "The Lord is my shepherd, I shall not want" (Ps. 23:1). Where all wealth abounds, there can be no want. "My God shall supply all your need" (Phil. 4:19). One God answers all needs, because one God includes all excellencies. He is a comprehensive good; in Him are all the treasures of heaven and earth, and infinitely more. "God of all comfort" is His name (2 Cor. 1:3). As all light is in the sun, so all comfort (or, all good) is in God. God is an ocean of all delights and blessings, without bank or bottom. He is the epitome of inconceivably more and incomparably better than all this world's delights.

"The God of hope fill you with all joy" (Rom. 15:13). (1) Here is joy. It is the cream of our desires and the overflowing of our delights. It is the sweet tranquility of our minds, the quiet repose of our hearts. As the sun to the flowers, it enlarges and cheers our affections. Joy is the target that everyone desires to hit. The philosopher well observed that joy is the dilation of the heart for its embracing of, closing with, and union to, its most beloved object. (2) Here is all joy. Variety adds to its luster and beauty. The Christian sits at a banquet made up of all sorts of rare and precious wines, and all manner of dainties and delicacies. He may walk in this garden, and delight himself with diversity of pleasant fruits and flowers. All joy! One kind of delight, like Mary's box of ointment (John 12:3), being opened, fills the whole house with its savor. If that is so, then what will all sorts of precious perfumes and fragrant ointments do? (3) Here is filling with all joy. Plenty of what is so exceedingly pleasant must necessarily enhance its price. There is not a crevice in the heart of a Christian into which this light does not enter. It is able to fill him (even if he were a far larger vessel than he is) up to the brim with this wine. The joy, arising from the creature, is an empty joy, but this is a satisfying joy: "Fill you with all joy" (Rom. 15:13). (4) He is God, who gives all joy. On what root does such a variety of luscious fruit grow? It does not spring out of the earth. Its fountain is in heaven: "The God of hope fill you with all joy" (Rom. 15:13). The vessel of the creature is full of dregs. It can never produce such choice delights. This pure river of the water of life proceeds only from the throne of God (Rev. 22:1).

CHAPTER 11

God Alone Is Suitable to Man's Soul

This delight and joy in God also arises from His suitableness to the nature of heaven-born saints. In other words, God is a proportional good. That which makes a man happy must be suitable to his spiritual soul. All satisfaction arises from some likeness between the faculty and the object. The cause of our pleasure in food is the suitableness of our taste to that which is in our food. Silver does not satisfy someone who is sick, and raiment does not satisfy someone who is hungry. Why? These are not answerable to the particular needs of nature.

The prince of philosophers (Aristotle) observes that the creatures are only satisfied by those things that are accommodated to their various natures. The birds, beasts, and fish live upon, and delight in, that food which is suitable to their distinct beings. The ox feeds on grass, the lion on meat, and the goat on branches. Some animals live on dew, some on fruit, and some on weeds. Some creatures live in the air while others live in the water. The mole and worm choose the earth, while the salamander chooses the fire. In the same plant, the bee feeds on the flower, the bird on the seed, the sheep on the blade, and the swine on the root. What is the reason for all this? Nature must find its rest and delight in that which is suitable to its own appetite and desire.

It is for this reason that God, although He is so perfect a good, is not the happiness of evil men or evil angels. He is not suitable to their depraved natures. The devils are as contrary to God's nature as fire is to water. The carnal mind, which bears sway in unregenerate men, is at enmity with God (Rom. 8:7). Only spiritual men, therefore, will enjoy happiness in the Father of spirits. He is the savory meat that their souls love. The sinner can live upon dregs, as the swine lives upon dung, but the saint must have refined spirits, and nothing less than angels' food and delights.

It is an unquestionable truth that nothing can give true comfort to man except that which has a relation and bears a proportion to his highest and noblest part—his immortal soul. His sensitive faculties were created in him to be subordinate and serviceable to their master—reason. The eagle excels all in seeing and the hound excels all in scenting, but man excels all in his rational soul. Only the blessed God is a suitable good to the heavenly, spiritual soul of man. Only God can satisfy it. Philosophers tell us that the reason why iron cleaves to the loadstone is because the pores of both are alike; as a result, there are outflows and emanations that slide through them and unite them together. One cause of the saint's love for, and delight in, God is his likeness to God. Creatures are earthly, but the soul is heavenly. Creatures are corporeal, but the soul is spiritual. Therefore, like friends who are contrary in disposition, the soul cannot find its rest and happiness in the fruition of creatures. God alone is suitable, and therefore satisfying: "I am the Almighty God" (Gen. 17:1). As the breast is suitable to the baby, and nothing else will quiet him, so God is suitable to His children.

A man who is hungry finds his stomach craving food. If you give him music, company, pictures, houses, and honors, he is not satisfied. Why? These are not suitable to his appetite—his stomach still craves more. However, if you set some wholesome food before this man, and let him eat, his craving will subside. "They did eat, and were filled" (Neh. 9:25). So it is with man's soul. His soul is full of cravings and longings, spending itself in pursuit of its proper food. If you give it the credit, profits, and pleasures of the world, his desire is not abated. He still craves, because these things do not answer the soul's nature, and therefore cannot answer its need. However, if you set God before man's soul, and it feeds on Him, it will be satisfied. Its inordinate appetite after the world will be cured. Having tasted this manna, it will trample on the onions of Egypt: "Whosoever drinketh of this water shall thirst again: but whosoever drinketh of the water that I shall give him shall never thirst" (John 4:14).

CHAPTER 12

God Alone Is Immortal Like Man's Soul

God is a permanent good. That which makes man happy must be immortal like man. Because man is rational, he is a prudent creature, desirous to prepare for the hereafter. This desire reaches far beyond that of the fool's, and extends to eternal life. He naturally desires an immortality of being, and therefore an eternity of blessedness. The soul cannot enjoy any perfection of happiness unless it is proportionate to its own duration, for the greater our joy is in the fruition of any good, the greater our grief in its omission. Eternity is one of the fairest flowers in the glorified saint's garland of honor. It is an eternal weight of glory (2 Cor. 4:17). Were the triumphant spirits ever to put off their crown of life, the very thought of it would be death to them, and, like leaven, it would sour the whole lump of their comforts. The perpetuity of their state adds infinitely to their pleasure, "We shall ever be with the Lord" (1 Thess. 4:17). While here, they have many sweet enticements, but once there, God will be their eternal dish—never absent from the heavenly table.

The creature cannot make man happy, because it is not able to fill him nor is it able to remain with him. Like the moon, it may shine a little at night, but it is gone by morning. Man cannot even be certain that he will enjoy the creature while he lives. How often is the candle of outward comforts blown out by a sudden blast of providence! Like Naomi (Ruth 1:21), many go out full, but return home empty. Some disaster, like a thief, meets them on the way, and robs them of their deified treasure. While the ship in which many men store their wealth dances along with its proud sails upon the surging waters, man pleases himself with the thoughts of favor he will receive from his merchant for making so profitable a voyage. However, in an instant, his ship is swallowed up by unseen quicksand. His freight is delivered at another port to an unknown master. Many, whose morning has been sunny and clear, have encountered storms before nightfall. These have washed their wealth away.

Even if these comforts do manage to continue all day, they leave us at the night of death. They are like a knife that stabs the sinner to the heart, letting out the blood of all his joy and happiness.

God, however, is the true happiness of the soul, because He is an eternal good. This Sun has no mists, and it never sets. Therefore, the rest of the soul in God is an eternal Sabbath. It is like the New Jerusalem, knowing no night. Earthly comforts, in which most people place their happiness, are like land-floods that swell, making a great noise, but are quickly gone. The blessed God, however, is like a springhead that runs over and runs forever.

The fact that God is a perfect, suitable, and eternal good is of little comfort to those who have no interest in Him. Another man's health will not make me happy when I am sick. What happiness does a beggar have in an earl's shady walkways, pleasant gardens, stately buildings, beautiful rooms, costly furniture, and precious jewels, when none of it belongs to him? A crown and scepter are as suitable to the nature of a subject as a sovereign, but they do not extend any comfort to the former, because they do not belong to him. The absence of one word in a will may mar the estate and disappoint a man's hopes. Likewise, the absence of this one word, *my* (in *my* God), is the wicked man's loss of heaven. The dagger will pierce his heart in hell for all eternity.

The degree of satisfaction in any good is according to the degree of our union to it. Hence, the saint's joy is greater in God in the other world than in this world, because there the union is nearer. However, where there is no ownership there is no union, and therefore there is no satisfaction. Now, this all-sufficient, suitable, and eternal God is the saint's peculiar portion, and therefore causes infinite satisfaction: "God is my portion forever. God, even our own God, shall bless us" (Ps. 67:6). The pronoun *my* is worth as much to the soul as the boundless portion. All our comfort is locked up in that private cabinet. Wine in the glass does not cheer the heart unless it is consumed. The psalmist's interest in God is the mouth whereby he feeds on those dainties that so exceedingly delight him. No love potion has ever been as effectual as this pronoun.

When God says to the soul, as Ahab to Benhadad, "Behold, I am thine, and all that I have" (1 Kings 20:4), it leaps with joy, and almost expires in longing after Him! Others, like strangers, may behold His honor and excellence; but only the saint, like a wife, enjoys Him. Luther says, "Much religion lies in pronouns." All our consolation, indeed, consists in this pronoun. The cup holds all our pleasant waters.

I will undertake to declare these two words, *my God*. All the joys of the believer hang upon this one string. If you break it, all is lost. I have sometimes thought of how David rolls it like a lump of sugar under his tongue, as one who is afraid to lose its sweetness too soon, "I will love thee, O LORD, my strength. The LORD is my rock, and my fortress, and my deliverer; my God, my strength, in whom I will trust; my buckler, and the horn of my salvation, and my high tower" (Ps. 18:1–2). This pronoun is the door at which the King of saints enters into our hearts with His whole train of delights and comforts.

CHAPTER 13

The Condition of Distressed Sinners and Saints

If the comfort of a Christian in his saddest condition is that God is his portion, it informs us of the difference between a sinner and a saint in terms of their condition when trouble comes.

The saint, in the sharpest winter, sits at a good fire. When abused by strangers, he can complain to, and comfort himself in, his Father. Although stars vanish out of sight, he can rejoice in the sun. "When thou passest through the waters, I will be with thee" (Isa. 43:2). In marked contrast, the sinner has no cover when a storm breaks over his head. When a foreboding grips his heart, he has no comfort, because he has no God. "Strangers from the covenants of promise, having no hope, and without God in the world" (Eph. 2:12). A godless man is hopeless. If he is robbed of his estate, and has little in hand, his case is dreadful, for he has even less in hope. God's promises are clefts of the rock where doves fly, and places of shelter, where doves are safe from birds of prey. However, the sinner is a stranger to these promises. When the floods come, he has no ark. Rather, he sinks like lead in the midst of the mighty waters.

The godly man, in the lowest ebb of creature enjoyment, may have a high tide of comfort, because he always has the God of all consolation. In the greatest outward famine, God entertains His people at His own table. Surely, it is neither poor nor sparing! As their afflictions abound, their consolations in Christ superabound (2 Cor. 1:5). The world lays on crosses and Christ lays on comforts. Men make grievous sores and God provides precious ointments. "The Lord is my portion, saith my soul; therefore will I hope in him" (Lam. 3:24). If you observe the context, you will admire the church's solace. The whole book of Lamentations is a pathetic description of her tragic condition. It is generally believed to have been written by Jeremiah in the time of the Babylonian captivity, when her land was wasted, her people enslaved, her Sabbaths ceased, and her temple profaned. Nevertheless, in the midst of this hard winter, he declares, "The Lord is my portion, saith my soul; therefore will I hope in him" (Lam. 3:24).

The godly man may be robbed of his possessions, but he is still well, because he has his happiness—his portion. The prophet Habakkuk, when the ponds were dried up, fetched his water from the fountain: "Although the fig tree shall not blossom, neither shall fruit be in the vines; the labor of the olive shall fail, and the fields shall yield no meat; the flock shall be cut off from the fold, and there shall be no herd in the stalls: yet will I rejoice in the LORD, I will joy in the God of my salvation" (Hab. 3:17–18). It is highly significant that he speaks not only of the loss of things of convenience (e.g., the vine and fig tree) but things of necessity (e.g., the meat of the field and the flock of the fold). In the absence of such comforts of life, he supports himself with God, who is the life of all his comforts.

However, the ungodly man is not like this. When afflictions come, they strike him in full, because he lacks armor. He is like a naked man in the midst of venomous serpents and stinging scorpions. When trouble comes like a pride of lions, it tears him (a silly lamb) in pieces, because there is nothing to protect him. "I am sore distressed," says Saul, "for the Philistines make war against me, and God is departed from me" (1 Sam. 28:15). Oh, poor soul! If the Philistines had been his burden, and if God had strengthened his back, then all would have been well! However, because his enemies approached and God had departed, Saul is greatly distressed.

The man who stands in the open field, where bullets fly thick and fast, without any shelter or defense, should be full of frights and fears. David's foes would have achieved their end, if their assertion had been true: "Persecute and take him; for God hath forsaken him" (Ps. 71:11). When God leaves a man, dangers and devils will quickly find him. Is it any wonder that Micah cries out so mournfully at the loss of his false gods, "Ye have taken away my gods…what is this that ye say unto me, What aileth thee?" (Judg. 18:24). How much more will the loss of the true God make men mournful. As it was said of Coniah, "Write ye this man childless" (Jer. 22:30), it may be said of every godless man, "Write this man comfortless, helpless, and hopeless forever!"

The difference between the case of the good and bad in distress is vast. The former keeps his color in all weather. The latter, like a leaf, trembles at the smallest wind. Naturalists observe the following difference between eagles and other birds. When birds are in distress, they make a pitiful noise. The eagle, on the other hand, when in difficulty, does not make any mournful sound, but mounts higher and refreshes herself in the warm beams of the sun. Saints, like true eagles, when they are in necessity, mount up to God upon the wings of faith and prayer, and delight themselves with the golden rays and gracious influences of His favor. However, the sinner, when deprived of outward comforts, mournfully complains. If you remove the snail from his shell, it dies.

When the barbarians plundered Paulinus Molanus's city, he declared, "Lord, why should I be disquieted for my silver and gold? Thou art to me all things." Likewise, the godly man, having nothing, possesses all things (2 Cor. 6:10).

CHAPTER 14

The Portion of Distressed Sinners and Saints

The wicked man has a portion of goods: "Father, give me the portion of goods that falleth to me" (Luke 15:12). However, the godly man has the good portion. I will show in three details how the portion of a sinner in this world differs from that of a saint.

1. The Sinner's Portion Is Poor

The sinner's portion consists of toys and trifles. Sinners are like those women in the city, who make a great noise in advertising their pins and matches. However, the portion of a saint, even though he does not proclaim it in the streets, lies in staple commodities and jewels. The worldly person's portion is at best a little airy honor, empty pleasure, or beggarly treasure. However, the Christian's portion is the beautiful image of God, the incomparable covenant of grace, the exceedingly rich and precious promises of the gospel, the inestimable Savior, and the infinitely blessed God. The sinner's portion is nothing: "Ye have rejoiced in a thing of nought" (Amos 6:13). It is a passing fashion or fancy (Acts 25:23; 1 Cor. 7:30). However, the saint's portion is all things: "All things are yours...and ye are Christ's; and Christ is God's" (1 Cor. 3:21–23).

Abraham gave gifts to the sons of his concubines, and sent them away, but he gave all he had to Isaac. Likewise, God gives common gifts of riches, friends, and credit, to wicked men (which is all they crave), and sends them away, but He gives grace, glory, His Spirit, His Son, Himself, all He has, to His Isaacs, to the children of promise (Gen. 25:5–6). He puts earth into the hands of the wicked (Job 9:24). All their portion lies in dust and rubbish. All they are worth is a few ears of corn, which they glean here and there in the field of this world. However, God puts heaven into the hearts of the godly. Their portion consists in gold, silver, diamonds, the peculiar treasure of kings, the love of God, the blood of Christ, and the pleasures at His right hand forevermore.

Sinners, like servants, have a little meat, drink, and wages. However, saints, like sons, are a congregation of the firstborn, and have the inheritance. Oh, the vast difference between the portion of the prodigal and the pious! The former has something given to him by God, but eventually it will appear to be little better than nothing. However, the latter has a good, worthy portion, because God loves him.

2. The Sinner's Portion Is Piercing

The sinner's portion is compared to broken cisterns for its vanity and to thorns for its vexation (Jer. 2:13; Matt. 13:22). A sinner lays the heavy lumber of his earthly portion upon his heart, and it oppresses him with cares, fears, and many sorrows. However, the saint's portion, the fine linen of his Savior's righteousness, is soft and pleasing.

"The abundance of the rich will not suffer him to sleep" (Eccl. 5:12). His portion hinders his peace, and his riches set him upon a rack. His cruelty in getting it, his care in increasing it, and the secret curse of God that accompanies it, allow him no rest day or night. However, the godly man's portion makes his bed easy, his pillow soft, and his covers warm. "I will both lay me down in peace, and sleep: for thou, LORD, only makest me dwell in safety" (Ps. 4:8). Such an excellent sleeping pill is this portion that, by the virtue of it, David, when he was pursued by his unnatural son and was in constant danger of death, when he had the earth for his bed, the trees for his curtains, the stars for his candles, and the heavens for his canopy, could sleep as sweetly and soundly as he ever did on his comfortable bed in his royal palace at Jerusalem. "Thou, O LORD, art a shield for me: my glory, and the lifter up of mine head" (Ps. 3:3).

The sinner's portion is called *wind* (Hos. 8:7). His riches, honors, and friends are within him, and therefore cause much anxiety and turmoil of soul. His portion is like smoke in his eyes, gravel in his teeth, wind in his stomach, and pain in his bowels. However, the saint's portion is his joy and delight. "Then will I go unto the altar of God, unto God my exceeding joy" (Ps. 43:4). It is music to his ears, beauty to his eyes, sweet odors to his scent, honey to his taste, and melody to his heart. In the presence of his portion "is fullness of joy," and at His right hand "are pleasures for evermore" (Ps. 16:11). He sits at an inward heart-cheering feast during the greatest outward famine. The worldly man, in the midst of his gaudy show of wealth, is a book with an ornate cover, consisting of nothing but tragedies. His portion is too narrow a garment to wrap himself in it, and too short a bed to stretch himself on it.

The vanity of the sinner's portion makes it full of vexation to him. Because it cannot fill him, it frets him. "In the fullness of his sufficiency he shall be in straits" (Job 20:22). Although his table is well spread, he has no heart to use it. Rather, he worries himself with fear of poverty. He runs here and there, up and down like a beggar, to this and that door of the creature, for some poor scraps. He may possess many millions, and not enjoy one penny (Eccl. 6:2).

However, the portion of the saint grants him a comfortable living. He does not receive the whole until he comes to full age, yet the interest alone (which is provided at present), gives him such an honorable allowance that he does not need to borrow from his servants nor become indebted to his beggarly neighbors. He has enough to live upon, and therefore he no longer walks to the creature's shop to meet his needs.

3. The Sinner's Portion Is Perishing

This fire of thorns, at which carnal men warm their hands (for it cannot reach the heart), goes out after a small blaze and a little blustering noise. Like comets, carnal comforts appear for a time, and then vanish. However, the portion of a saint, like a true star, is fixed and firm. A worldly man's wealth lies in the earth, and therefore it decays and grows moldy like goods stored in a damp cellar. However, the godly man's treasure is in heaven. As goods stored in a dry room, it continues safe. Earthly portions are like guests, who stay for a night and then depart. However, the saint's portion is an inhabitant that abides in the house forever.

It is said of Gregory the Great that he trembled every time he read or thought of those words of Abraham to Dives, "Son, remember that thou in thy lifetime receivedst thy good things" (Luke 16:25). Oh, what joy to have all in time, and nothing when entering eternity! Oh, what joy to live like a prodigal for one day, and be a beggar forever! The flower sheds while the stalk remains. Likewise, the sinner continues when his portion vanishes. When the sinner dies, his portion, like his servant, will seek a new master. "Thou fool, this night thy soul shall be required of thee: and then whose shall those things be?" (Luke. 12:20). Whose? It may go to the poor, whom he had wronged and robbed to enrich himself. It may go to his children, who will scatter it as wastefully as he collected it greedily. Whoever gets it, the point is this: it will not be his. When parted from his portion, what a poor fool was he indeed! He was not worth a penny. However, the saint's wealth will accompany him into the other world. Truly, that is the place where he will receive his full portion. "Blessed are the dead which die in the Lord...they may rest from their labors; and their works do follow them" (Rev. 14:13).

When men embark on a great journey beyond the sea, they do not carry their tables, or beds, or any heavy luggage that will burden them along the way. They carry their silver, gold, and jewels. When the sinner goes the way of all the earth, he leaves his portion behind him, because it consists entirely of furniture. However, the saint's portion consists entirely of things of value: in wisdom, which is better than silver; in grace, which is worth more than pure gold; and in God, who is more precious than rubies. All that can be desired is not to be compared to God!

It is said of Dathan and his companions that the earth swallowed them, their houses, and all that belonged to them (Num. 16:33). At death, when the earth swallows up the sinner's person, it will also swallow up his portion. This whole world must pass away. What then will become of the sinner's portion? Surely, he will cry out, as they of Moab, "Woe to me! I am undone" (Num. 21:29). It is as sad a statement as any in Scripture: "whose portion is in this life" (Ps. 17:14). However, at that day, the saint will sing and rejoice, for then he will know the full value of his inheritance.

CHAPTER 15

The Portion of Sinners and Saints in the World to Come

There is another difference between the portion of a sinner and saint: the worse it is for the one and the better it is for the other in the other world.

The sinner's portion here, as poor as it is, is a comparative heaven. There, it will be a real hell. Their portion is cursed on earth, but what will it be in hell? "Upon the wicked he shall rain snares, fire and brimstone, and an horrible tempest: this shall be the portion of their cup" (Ps. 11:6). The words are an allusion to the Jewish custom at meals whereby everyone had an allotted portion of drink—his peculiar cup (Gen. 43:34). The godly man can tell you what nectar he will enjoy when he sits down at that eternal banquet: "The LORD is the portion of mine inheritance and of my cup: thou maintainest my lot" (Ps. 16:5).

Look a little into the sinner's cup, and see what a bitter potion is prepared for him! It is infinitely worse than poison. Reader, take heed that you never taste it! It is indeed a mixture of such ingredients that it will make the stoutest heart to tremble and faint, if it comes merely within the scent or sight of it—snares, fire, brimstone, and a horrible tempest! The Lord pours out on the Egyptians such a "grievous hail, such as hath not been in Egypt since the foundation thereof" (Ex. 9:18). However, the portion of the sinner is far more bitter than that plague!

1. The Extremity of the Pain

First, observe the extremity of the pain. "Upon the wicked he shall rain fire and brimstone" (Ps. 11:6). Fire is dreadful to our flesh. What miserable torment did Charles the Second, king of Navarre, endure when he was burnt to death in a flaming sheet! That is merely an outward application. How much greater torment will fire cause when applied inwardly! The inward parts are more tender, and therefore more liable to torture. However, this drink, like poison, will diffuse itself into all the parts. None will be free from pain.

It was a terrible punishment which the drunken Turk underwent, when he had a cup of boiling lead poured down his throat. Who can imagine what he felt? As bad as it was, I am certain that it was merely a flea-bite in comparison to the cup of fire that the Lord has prepared for the sinner—fire and brimstone! Fire is terrible in and of itself, but brimstone makes it burn with much greater violence. At present, the sinner burns in lust, but then in a flaming fire. At present, he drinks pleasant juices, but then a loathsome potion. Fire is the most furious of all elements. Nothing in this life is more dreadful to nature. However, our fires are like painted ones in comparison to this rain of fire in hell. Nebuchadnezzar's furnace (Dan. 3:19), although heated seven times more than ordinary, was cool compared to this fire! Oh, who can fry in a flame, kindled by the breath of an infinite God? Fire and brimstone! Three drops of brimstone, touching any part of our bodies, will make us cry and roar with pain. What then will befall the sinner when he will live forever in this lake of fire and brimstone? What then will befall the sinner when he will drink this bottomless cup of pure wrath, poisonous dregs, fire, and brimstone? "Who among us shall dwell with everlasting burnings?" (Isa. 33:14).

2. The Certainty of the Punishment

Second, observe the certainty of the punishment. "Upon the wicked he shall rain…an horrible tempest" (Ps. 11:6). A blasting whirlwind destroys everything in its path. It burns whatever it touches. The sinner thinks that he is safe, but this horrible tempest will overrun him. His queasy stomach, accustomed to rich wines, grows nauseous from this loathsome, nasty drink. When God puts this cup into his hand, his heart rises against it. However, he will be forced to drink this cup of fire and boiling brimstone!

3. The Suddenness of the Plague

Third, observe the suddenness of the plague. "Upon the wicked he shall rain snares" (Ps. 11:6). While they are sleeping and not even dreaming about it, this horrible tempest will steal them away in the night (Job 27:20). What a miserable screech and dreadful cry will this cause, as among the Egyptians at midnight (Ex. 12:30)! Traps ensnare men unaware. The sinner's woe will come without warning. "As the fishes that are taken in an evil net, and as birds that are caught in the snare; so are the sons of men snared in an evil time, when it falleth suddenly upon them" (Eccl. 9:12). The fish is busy looking for good bait, when the hook catches it. The bird is expecting meat in the snare, when it is trapped and killed. When Abner expects a kiss and warm greeting, he meets with a sword that kills him (2 Sam. 3:27–30). When the sinner, like the dolphin, is leaping merrily, then he is closest to his endless misery. "Upon the wicked he shall rain snares" (Ps. 11:6). When it rains, the sinner expects silver showers to refresh him, but it drops snares to entrap him. The wicked man's cloud does not drop blessing, but fire and fury.

Let us draw up an account to see how much the worldly man's portion is worth, and how much it will be worth in the other world. The liquor in his cup is most painful and loathsome—fire and brimstone! All his estate lies in the valley of the shadow of death. It would be a wonderful favor, if he were to drink scalding lead instead of boiling brimstone. No one can conceive how terrible a potion it is, that God—who is boundless in wisdom, power, and anger—prepares! If it were doubtful that it would happen, the sinner's grief would not be so great. However, it is most certain. God will pour this dreadful drink down his throat. The sinner cannot abide it, nor can he avoid it. Infinite power will hold him while infinite anger gives him this potion. This rain of fire and brimstone, which will cause such matchless mourning, will come when it is least expected, after a sunny morning.

4. The Perpetuity of the Suffering

There is one thing more in the cup which makes it infinitely bitter: it is bottomless (Luke 8:31). The sinner's fire is eternal, and the smoke of his brimstone ascends forever (Rev. 14:11). If a purging potion, which is soon swallowed and passed through the body, causes a man so much displeasure, what will he experience when he drinks this bottomless cup of fire and brimstone! His cup is like the ocean that can never be fathomed. This rain is called "wrath to come," for it is forever to come and never overcome. The sinner's darkest night here has a morning, but his portion there will be darkness forever! There will be no end of his misery and no escape from his tragedy. He will be bound in chains of everlasting darkness, and he will feel the terrors of an eternal death.

However, the portion of a saint is, like the wine that Christ provided for the wedding (John 2:1–11), best at the last. The saint will never know its full worth until he appears in the other world. Then he will discover that his portion will protect him from all misery, and fill him with abundant happiness, and answer all the desires and needs of his capacious and immortal soul.

The cup which he will drink is filled from the rivers of God's own pleasures. How sweet is that wine? None can tell, but those who have tasted it. The mere thought of it has restored those who were dying. What will a swallow of it do? No men in the world can describe the rich and various dainties that God has provided for His own people. Even the most skillful cherubim cannot calculate the total of a saint's personal estate. Until angels can acquaint us with the vast millions that the boundless God is worth, they cannot tell us the worth of our portion.

It is said that the city of Susa, in Persia, was so rich that its stones were joined together with gold, and that Alexander found seventy thousand talents of gold in it. However, what a beggarly place is this, compared to the New Jerusalem, where the roads are pure gold and the walls are precious pearls! The infinite God—as boundless and good as He is, and to whom heaven and earth are less than nothing—is the saint's portion forever. More of this is discussed in the following chapters.

CHAPTER 16

Is God Your Joy?

The doctrine is also useful by way of trial. If the comfort of a Christian in his saddest condition is that God is his portion, then, reader, examine yourself to see whether God is your portion or not! I must tell you that the essence of religion consists in the choice of your portion. Furthermore, your happiness depends entirely upon your taking the blessed God for your utmost end and chiefest good. If you err here, you are lost forever.

I will test you very briefly by the standard that Christ has prepared: "Where your treasure is, there will your heart be also" (Matt. 6:21). Now, friend, where is your heart? Is it in earth? Is it a diamond set in lead or a sparkling star fixed in heaven? Are your greatest affections among the rubbish of this world or do they ascend the mount to converse with God? Do they, with the worms, crawl here below or do they, like the eagle, soar and dwell above? A man who has his portion on earth moves downward like the earth. He may, like a stone, be thrown upward occasionally by some sudden conviction, but that impression soon dwindles, and he falls again to earth. However, he who has his portion in heaven moves upward. Because of the violence of temptation, he may (as fire by the wind) be forced downward on occasion. Yet, once the temptation is removed, he moves upward again.

It may be that, when your enemy, death, beats you out of the battlefield of life, you will be glad to find a God to whom you may retreat, as a city of refuge, to shelter you from the murdering gun of the law's curse. However, what thoughts do you have of Him right now, when you have the world before you? Do you count the fruition of Him your chiefest felicity? Is one God infinitely weightier in the scales of your judgment than millions of worlds? In your prevailing judgment, are you able to say, "Happy is that people, that is in such a case [full harvests and fruitful flocks]"; but even more so, "Happy is that people, whose God is the Lord" (Ps. 144:13–15)?

Every man esteems his portion at a high price. Naboth values his earthly inheritance above his life. He would rather die than part with it for any price. "The LORD forbid it me that I should give the inheritance of my fathers unto thee" (1 Kings 21:3). Oh, great is the worth of the blessed God, in the estimation of him that has Christ for his portion! His house, land, wife, child, liberty, and life, are nothing to him in comparison to his portion in God. He would not exchange his hope of it, and title to it, for the dominion and sovereignty of the whole world. If the devil were to set him, as he did

Christ (Matt. 4:8–9), on the mount, and show him all the honors, pleasures, and treasures of the world, and say to him, "All this I will give you, if you will sell your portion, fall down, and worship me," he would reject the devil's offer with infinite disdain. This man is elevated to the top of the celestial orbs, and therefore the whole earth is but a speck in his sight. However, a man who has his portion in outward and earthly things does not value heavenly things. To him, the glorious sun itself is but small. In such a man's eye, earthly things are great.

Reader, it is important that you ask your soul two or three questions.

1. In What Channel Does the Stream of Your Desires Run?

In what direction do the winds of your soul drive you? Is it towards God, or towards the world? A rich heir, still in his minority, governed by tutors and guardians, longs for the time when he will be of age to enjoy the privileges and pleasures of his inheritance. You crave, thirst, long, and desire. There is something that you want to have, and must have, and cannot be satisfied until you have it. Now, what is it? Is it the husks of this world that you desire so earnestly for someone to give to you or is it bread in your Father's house that you hunger after? Do you pant after the dust of the earth (Amos 2:7)? Do you pant with the church: "The desire of our soul is to thy name, and to the remembrance of thee" (Isa. 26:8)? You are hungry, thirsty, disquieted, and unsatisfied. What is the matter, man? Is the voice of your heart, "Who will shew us any good? Lord, lift thou up the light of thy countenance upon us" (Ps. 4:6)?

Physicians can determine a great deal about the state of their patient's body by his appetite. Those who long for trash show that their stomachs are foul. Those who hunger after wholesome food are esteemed to be in health. You may judge the state of your soul by your desires. If you chiefly desire the trash of the world, then your spiritual state is not right, and your heart is not right in the sight of God. However, if you can say with David, "Whom have I in heaven but thee? And there is none upon earth that I desire beside thee" (Ps. 73:25), then you are blessed of the Lord! You have a part in this boundless portion. Observe, therefore, friend, which way the wings of your soul, your desires, fly! He who thirsts after the temporal water of this world has no right to the pure river of the water of life. However, he who hungers after the dainties of the Lamb's supper may be sure that the scraps of this beggarly world are not his happiness. The true wife longs for the return of her husband, but the false wife does not care how long he is absent.

2. At What Feast Do You Sit with Most Delight?

Do you sit at a table furnished with the comforts of this world? Are the dishes of credit and profit, relations and possessions, what you feed on with most pleasure? Alternatively, is it a table spread with the image of God, the favor of God, the Spirit of God, and the Son of God? Are those the savory meats that your soul loves?

If this Sun of righteousness causes day in your heart when He arises, and if, when He sets, it is still night with you, then God is your portion. Oh, how glad is the young heir when he comes to enjoy his portion! With what delight will he look over his woods, view his grounds, and walk in his gardens! Out of delight, some men tumble naked in their heaps of silver. However, if your affections only overflow with joy when the world flows in upon you, as the water of the Nile in the time of wheat harvest, then the world is your portion.

He, who, like a lark, sings merrily when he is mounting up to heaven, is rich indeed. God is his! However, he who, like a horsefly, delights in earthly dunghills, is a poor man. God is not his God! It is an undeniable truth that our portion is whatever the paradise of our pleasures is. The fool, who expected ease on his bed of thorns—"Soul, thou hast much goods laid up for many years; take thine ease" (Luke 12:19)—had his portion in this life. However, Moses could not be pleased by anything but God's gracious presence as his portion. "If thy presence go not with me, carry us not up hence.... I beseech thee, shew me thy glory" (Ex. 33:15, 18).

3. What Calling Do You Follow with Greatest Eagerness and Earnestness?

Men run and ride, toil, and labor, rise early and retire

late, and exert great effort for whatever they regard as their happiness and portion. The worldly man, whose portion consists, like the peddler's pack, in a few pins, needles, spoons, or buttons, eats poorly, sleeps intermittently, and hazards his health, life, and soul for that which he counts his portion. Like a spaniel, he will follow his master, the world, hundreds of miles, puffing and blowing, breaking through hedges, scratching himself with thorns and briers, running through ponds of water and puddles of dirt, and all for a few bones or scraps. This is all his hope and happiness.

The Christian, who has the blessed God for his portion, strives, labors, watches, prays, weeps, and thinks no time too much, no pains too great, and no cost too high for the enjoyment of his God. As the wise merchant, he will part with all he has, all his strength, and health, all his relations and possessions, for his noble portion. Reader, how is it with you? You travel back and forth. You weary yourself. You lack rest. Your head is full of cares and your heart is full of fears. Your hands are always active. However, for what purpose are they active? To what market are you walking so fast? Is it gold that you pursue so frantically? "The people shall labor in the very fire, and the people shall weary themselves for very vanity" (Hab. 2:13). Is it God that you seek? "My soul followeth hard after thee" (Ps. 63:8).

I have briefly laid down the character of those who have God as their portion. Your business is to be faithful in examining your state. If you find that God is your portion, rejoice in your privilege, and let your practice be consistent. Like a rich heir, delight yourself in the thoughts of your vast inheritance. Can the one who is master of the mint be poor? Can you be miserable when you have God for your portion? I must tell you that you are happy in spite of men and devils. If worldly men take such pleasure in their accounts and investments, what joy may you have in God? If all the gold of the whole world were melted into one stream, and if all the pearls and precious stones were set on the banks of the stream, and if the excellencies of all other creatures were crushed into sand at the bottom of the stream, it would still be an unworthy metaphor for setting forth the least perfection in our portion—God!

Will you complain, as if you were pinched with poverty, when the boundless God is your portion? Are you not an unreasonable creature? Shame on you, Christian; mind yourself! Let the world know, by your cheerfulness and comfort, that their pennies are nothing to your millions! Even if the whole world should become bankrupt, you are rich, because your estate does not lie in their hands. Do not sulk, therefore, with fear of poverty. However, keep a house as your estate will afford it, in the greatest plenty!

Let your practice be consistent with your portion. Great heirs behave themselves in a different manner than the poor, who take alms from the parish. You ought to live above the world. Eagles must not stoop to catch flies. You, who are so near to God, should not wander about this world, but should live as one whose hope and happiness is in a better world. When a man was asked whether he admired the admirable structure of some stately building, he replied, "No, for I have been to Rome, where better buildings are seen every day." If the world tempts you with its rare sights and curious pleasures, you may scorn them. Having been in heaven, you are able by faith to see infinitely better every hour of the day.

However, if, upon examination, it is discovered that God is not your portion, think of this seriously: you are but a beggar! In addition, if you die in this state, you will be a beggar forever! It may be that you are worth millions in this world, but, alas, they stand for nothing in the other world. How little will your bags of silver be worth when you enter your coffin! When you come to die, the whole world will be but air and smoke in your account. What, man, will you do? Where will you go? The God to whom you will cry out in distress, and before whom you will weep, sob, and sigh at death is not your God. You reject Him now, yet you think He will receive you then? You must make a new choice, or you can never enter into peace.

CHAPTER 17

Choose God as Your Treasure

The third use that I will make of this doctrine is by way of exhortation. If the comfort of a Christian in his saddest condition is that God is his portion, then let me urge you, reader, to choose God for your portion. I look on you as rational and, accordingly, I will deal with you as if reason were judge. I will prevail with you to repent of your former choice, and to resolve to make a new one.

You have chosen the world for your portion. However, have you not read of what a poor, pitiful, piercing, and perishing portion it is? "Wherefore do ye spend money for that which is not bread? And your labor for that which satisfieth not? Hearken diligently unto me, and eat ye that which is good, and let your soul delight itself in fatness" (Isa. 55:2). I offer you this day a portion that is worthy of your choicest affections. If you accept it, the richest emperors will be beggars in comparison to you. This portion contains more wealth than heaven and earth. Ten thousand worlds are nothing in comparison to this portion. If a man were to offer you a bag of gold, a bag of counters, a bag of pearls, or a bag of sand, which would you choose? Surely, you would choose the bag of gold! The world in comparison to God is infinitely less than brass is to gold, or sand is to pearls. Will you not choose Him for your portion?

Have you ever laughed at children for their folly in choosing toys and rattles instead of things of much greater worth? In addition, are you not a bigger child, and a greater fool, for choosing husks instead of bread, stew instead of the birthright? Are you not a greater fool for choosing an apparent fancy instead of real joy, a little honor (which is but a small candle that children can blow out with one breath) instead of the exceeding and eternal weight of glory? To choose broken cisterns instead of a fountain of living waters, dirt instead of diamonds, vanity instead of substance, drops instead of the ocean, and nothing instead of all things! Man, where is your reason?

Samuel said to Saul, "Set not thine mind on them [donkeys]...on whom is all the desire of Israel? Is it not on thee?" (1 Sam. 9:20). Friend, when you have the desire of all nations to set your heart upon, why would you set your heart on donkeys, flocks, shops, or any treasure? As Christ said to the woman of Canaan, "If thou knewest the gift of God, and who it is that saith to thee, Give me to drink; thou wouldest have asked of him, and he would have given thee living water" (John 4:10). So I say to you, "If you knew the blessed God, and who it is that is offered to you—the sweetest love, the richest mercy, the surest friend, the chiefest good, the greatest beauty, the highest honor, and the fullest happiness—you would leave the coal ships of this world to load themselves with thick clay, and turn merchant adventurer for the other world. You would be more willing to leave these frothy joys and a drossy delight for the enjoyment of God than any prisoner was ever willing to leave the chains and misery of jail for the liberty, pleasures, and preferment of a court."

Augustine speaks of a time when he and his mother were discussing the comforts of the Spirit: "Lord," says Augustine, "Thou knowest in that day how wisely we did esteem of the world, and all its delights." Oh, reader, if you were to see the vastness, suitableness, and fullness of this portion, I am confident that you would allow the natives of this world (Ps. 17:14) to seek the goods of their own country, and that you would seek your riches from another world!

The cause of your wrong choice is your ignorance of the worth and excellence of the object that I am offering to you. Knowledgeable people prefer wisdom over silver, gold, or rubies (Prov. 3:14–15). A man will sell his heart to the one who offers the most. Now, the devil offers the brutish pleasures of sin. The world offers treasures and honors, which are really vain, vexing, and perishing. However, God offers the precious blood of His Son, the curious embroidery of His Spirit, the noble employment and honorable advancement of angels, fullness of joy, and infiniteness of satisfaction, in the fruition of His blessed self to all eternity. Now, why is it that the devil's offer is accepted and the world's offer is embraced while God's offer (which is far more glorious, like the glorious heaven in comparison to the stinking dunghill) is rejected? Truly, the reason is this: Men do not know the worth of what God offers them for their heart. Swine trample on pearls, because they do not know their worth (Matt. 7:6). No one looks away from the world except those who are able to look beyond it.

The turtle, says the philosopher, brings forth blind hatchlings. Similarly, the most clear-sighted Christian brings forth blind children. Unable to see into the other world, they prefer these poor things, offered at present, to these unsearchable riches, offered in the future. For this reason, the devil, like the raven when he seizes a carcass, first pecks out the eyes of his victims (Prov. 30:17). The devil knows that, as soon as they see the blessed God and the happiness that is enjoyed in Him, they will quickly turn their backs on these shadows, and turn towards this eternal substance (2 Cor. 4:4).

Oh, how dull is the world's common glass in the eye of him who has seen the true crystal! The loadstone of earth will not draw away man's affections while this diamond of heaven is present. Once Moses saw Him who is invisible, the value of all the honors, treasures, and pleasures of Egypt fell in his judgment (Heb. 11:24–27). Knowledge is indeed appetite's taster, so that the one who has fed on the heavenly banquet cannot savor anything else.

A man who is born in a dark dungeon and stays there a long time, admires the excellence of a candle when he first sees it. What delight does he take in beholding it, and inquiring into the nature of it! However, if this same man enters the open air and beholds the glorious sun, his admiration for the candle quickly ceases. All his wonder is now focused on the beauty and glory of this great luminary of the world. Every man is naturally in darkness. For this reason, when he beholds the candles of creature comforts, he is ravished and allured by them. However, if he sees the Sun of righteousness, the all-sufficient and eternal God, he despises the glimmering of those candles, and wonders at the excellence and perfection of this glorious being. What was previously glorious now has no glory in comparison to this glory that excels all. All things are small and little in the eye of him who has had a glimpse of the great God. The great cities of Campania are but small cottages to them that stand on the top of the Alps.

Philosophers observe that light is the conveyor of heat. It is certain, reader, that this light of knowledge would quickly cause heat in your affections if you were to see God with an eye of faith. Your eye would so affect your heart that you would shut your eyes to all those gilded poisons and wink forever at all those specious nothings. If you were to see this God as He is visible in the glass of the creatures, if you were to encircle the earth and see the many islands and continents that are in it, if you were to surround the earth, like the sun, and see all the nations that are in it—their languages, carriages, customs, numbers, orders, and natures; if you were to see the various plants, birds, minerals, beasts, and savage inhabitants of wildernesses—variety, disposition, subordination, and service to each other, what thoughts would you then have of taking this God as your portion!

Oh, if you were to behold in one view the vast ocean, discern the motion of the huge waters in their ebbing and flowing, all the storms and tempests that are raised there, and all the persons and goods that are ruined there! Oh, if you were to see how those proud waves are calmed with a word, how they are held back with bars and doors, and how, for all their anger and power, they cannot go beyond their decreed place! Oh, if you were able to dive into the ocean and see the many wonders that are in that great deep, the vast riches that are buried out of the sight of covetous mortals! Oh, if you were to see the leviathan, whose teeth are terrible, whose scales are his pride, and whose sneezing gives forth light! His eyes are the eyelids of the morning, his breath kindles coals, he esteems iron as straw and brass as rotten wood, and he makes the deep to boil like a pot and the sea like a pot of ointment! Oh, if you were to behold the innumerable fish, both small and great, that are there, then what would you think of having the author and commander of the earth and ocean as your portion?

Oh, if you were to ascend to the sky, and perceive the beauty, glory, nature, and order of the heavenly host—how they march in rank and file, how they appear in their several courses when called, and how they know the time of their rising and setting! Oh, if you were to know the sun perfectly in its noonday dress, and what influences those higher orbs have on inferior bodies, what would you then give to enjoy Him, who gave them their beings, who appoints them their motions, who knows the number of the stars, and who calls them all by their names?

Oh, if it were possible for you to hold aside the veil, and look into the holy of holies, to mount up to the highest heavens, and see the royal palace of this great King, the stately court that He keeps, the noble entertainment that He provides for His friends and children! Oh, if you were to know the satisfying joy, the ravishing delight, and the inconceivable pleasure, which the souls of just men made perfect have in His favor and fruition! Oh, if you were to see Him as He is visible (like a pure sweet light, sparkling through a crystal) in the glorified Redeemer, and know Him as you are known of Him; then, then, reader, what would you think of taking this God as your portion?

Oh, what poor apprehensions would you have of that beggarly portion that you now admire! What dung, what dogs' meat would the world be to you in comparison to this God! When Alexander heard of the riches in the Indies, he left the kingdom of Macedonia to his captains. Likewise, if you were to see God with the eye of faith, you would leave the swine of the earth to wallow in the mire of brutish comforts, the foolish children of disobedience to paddle in the gutter of sensual waters, and you would desire that your portion might be among God's children, and your heritage among His chosen ones. Then, then, friend, you would think that all your love is too little, and no labor too great, for such a peerless and inestimable portion.

How earnestly, how eagerly would you cry with Moses, after he caught a glimpse of Canaan, "O Lord God, thou hast begun to shew thy servant thy greatness and thy mighty hand: for what God is there in heaven or in earth that can do according to thy works, and according to thy might? I pray thee, let me go over and see the good land that is beyond Jordan, that goodly mountain, and Lebanon" (Deut. 3:24–25). Lord, although others are put off with common bounty, let me partake of special mercy. Although they feed on husks, give me this bread of life. Let me not, for this whole world, have my portion in this world, but may Thou be the portion of my cup. Whatever Thou deniest me, or however Thou dealest with me, give me Thyself, and I will have enough. Although those, who are strangers and enemies to Thee, scramble for the good things that Thou scatterest here below and desire no more, yet let me see the felicity of Thy chosen, rejoice with the gladness of Thy nation, and glory with Thy inheritance! Oh, friend, it is eternal life to know this only true God, and Jesus Christ whom He has sent (John 17:3).

Were I able to set this God forth in the thousandth part of that grace and glory with which He is clothed, as with a garment, and were I able to present Him to you in any degree suitable to His vast perfections, and give you eyes to behold Him, it would be impossible for you not to choose Him for your portion. However, alas, no angels in heaven can draw Him at length! Surely, then, we, who are clogged with so much flesh, know even less of this Father of spirits. There is no finding God out, because there is no equal proportion between the faculty and the object. If I were to ascend to heaven, and see Him face to face, I would know Him to my perfection, but I could not know Him to His perfections. But suppose I were there, and saw those infinite beauties and glories, according to the utmost of my capacity, yet my tongue would still not be able to tell it to you, nor your ears to hear it. Oh, what an unspeakable loss I am at in describing this infinite God! My thoughts run into a maze or labyrinth. I am as a little boat floating on the ocean, or as an infant attempting to reach the sun.

Nevertheless, my meditations please me exceedingly. Oh, how sweet is this subject! I could dwell in this hive of honey and happiness. Lord, let me dwell here while I have a being! How pleasant are Thy thoughts to me! Oh, God, Thou art a true paradise of all pleasure, Thou, living fountain of felicity; Thou art the original and exact pattern of all perfections! How comely is Thy face, how lovely is Thy voice! While I behold but a little of Thy beauty and glory, my heart is filled with marrow and fatness, and my mouth praises Thee with joyful lips. My soul follows hard after Thee. Oh, when will I come and appear before Thee? When wilt Thou come to me or, rather, when will that blessed time come when I will be taken up to Thee?

Sinners reject Thee because they walk in the mist of ignorance. Did they know Thee, they would never crucify the Lord of glory! When they come into that blackness of darkness, where they will have light enough to see how good Thou art in Thyself and in Thy Son, and see their misery in the loss of an eternal blessed life, how they will tear their hair, bite their flesh, and cut their hearts with anguish and sorrow for their cruel folly and damnable, desperate madness in refusing so incomparable and inestimable a portion!

Saints bless themselves in Thee. They pity rather than envy the greatest potentates, who lack Thee for their portion. Having not seen Thee, they love Thee. Although they do not see Thee, yet believing, they rejoice with joy unspeakable and full of glory (1 Peter 1:8–9).

Alas, reader, I am wandering. I confess that I am a little out of the way. But I wish—as Augustine, who, when preaching, forgot his subject and began to prove the Manichees were wrong by which means Firmus was converted—that my going a few steps astray may be instrumental in bringing you home. What shall I say to you, or how will I persuade you? If it were possible for me, by my prayer, to move God to open your eyes, so that you could see the worth and worthiness, the love and loveliness, of this portion, you would not be alienated an hour longer from the life of God through the ignorance that is in you. But be of good comfort. Read on. He, who made the seeing eye, is willing to open the blind eye. Possibly, before you arrive at the end of this book, you will meet with the eye salve of the sanctuary that will do the necessary work.

CHAPTER 18

Satisfied and Sanctified

What I still have to offer you is to encourage you to choose God as your portion. It possesses four properties. In the handling of these, I will put the world in one scale with all its mines of gold, and I will put this one God in the other scale. Then, you must judge which scale is heaviest.

1. God Is a Satisfying Portion

The things of this world may oversupply a man, but they can never satisfy him. Most men have too much, but no man has enough. Like some ships, they hold cargo that sinks them when they actually have room to hold more. "He that loveth silver shall not be satisfied with silver, nor he that loveth abundance with increase" (Eccl. 5:10). Worldly men are like the Parthians, in that the more they drink, the more they thirst. The world cannot satisfy the senses, much less the soul. The eye is not satisfied with seeing, nor the ear with hearing.

There is a story of apes that found a glowworm on a frosty night, thought it was a spark of fire, gathered some sticks, and leaped on it, expecting to be warmed by it. All was in vain. So men think to find warmth and satisfaction in creatures, but they are like clothes to David when he was stricken in years—unable to give any heat. Where is contentment found? Where is the place of satisfaction? The sea says, "It is not in me." The earth says, "It is not in me." Heaven itself, were not God in it, would say, "It is not in me."

Reader, you long for the things of this world, and you think that if you could only have a table full of its dishes, you would feed heartily and fill yourself. However, do you not realize that they are like the meat that sick men desire? When it is brought to them, they can taste it, but they cannot fill themselves with it. The pond of the creature has so much mud at the bottom of it that no one can take a full draught of its water. The sun and moon seem bigger when they are rising than when they pass directly over our heads. All outward things are great in expectation, but nothing in realization.

The world promises as much and performs as little as the tomb of Semiramis. When she had built her stately tomb, she had this inscription placed on it: "Whatever king succeeds here and wants money, let him open this tomb, and he will have enough to serve his need." Darius, wanting money, opened the tomb. Instead of riches, he found this sharp reproof: "Unless you had been extremely covetous and greedy of filthy money, you would not have opened the grave of the dead to seek for it!" In this same way, many men run to the world with high hopes, but return with nothing but blanks. Hence it is that worldly men are said to feed on lies (Hos. 10:13; 12:1).

Reader, the controversy is so great among men. There are many who believe that rest grows on the furrows of the field, and that happiness dwells in the mines of gold. They believe that they can draw happiness out of the creature. For this reason, let us hear the judgment of a man who enjoyed the world at will, who had enough wisdom to extract the essence of it, and who set himself to examine all creation. Moreover, what does he say? "Vanity of vanities; all is vanity, saith the preacher" (Eccl. 12:8).

Mark the following: (1) The vanity of it: "vanity." This is vanity in the abstract. (2) The plurality of it: "vanity of vanities." It is excessive vanity, and nothing but vanity. (3) The universality of it: "all is vanity." This means all things individually, and all things collectively. Riches are vanity, honors are vanity, pleasures are vanity, knowledge is vanity—all is vanity! (4) The truth of it: "saith the preacher." He is one who speaks by experience, not hearsay. He is one who has tried the creature to the utmost, and found it to come far short of satisfying his desire. He is one who speaks by divine inspiration, not merely according to his own opinion. After he has added up all the creatures, the total is this: "Vanity of vanities, all is vanity, saith the preacher" (Eccl. 12:8).

Men who are in a valley, think that, if they were at the top of a hill, they would be able to touch the heavens. Men who are in the bottom of poverty, disgrace, or pain, think that, if they were to climb a mountain such as riches, honors, and delights, they would be able to reach happiness. Now, Solomon reached the top of this hill, and seeing so many others scrambling and laboring, even riding on one another's necks and pressing one another to death in order to get ahead, says to them, "Friends, you are all deceived in your expectations. I see the pain you take to climb up here, thinking that, when you get here, you will touch the heavens and reach happiness. However, I have arrived at the top of the hill ahead of you. I have treasures, honors, and pleasures in variety and abundance (Eccl. 2:12–13). In addition, I find the hill is full of bogs instead of delights. Instead of giving me satisfaction, it causes a great deal of trouble. Therefore, be advised to spare yourself, and use your strength for that which is truly profitable. Believe it; you labor in vain!" "Vanity of vanities, all is vanity, saith the preacher" (Eccl. 12:8).

We have weighed the world in the balance, and found it lighter than vanity. Now, let us see God's weight. David tells us that, even though the vessel of the creature is frozen and no satisfaction can be drawn out of it, this fountain (God) runs freely to the full contentment of all true Christians. "The LORD is the portion of mine inheritance and of my cup. Thou maintainest my lot" (Ps. 16:5). The former expression (as previously observed) is an allusion to the custom of dividing drink at banquets. The latter expression refers to the division of Canaan by lot and line (Ps. 78:55). Everyone's part was determined as the lot fell. Now, David's part and lot fell, like the Levites under the law, on God. Is he pleased in his portion? Can he take any delight in his estate? "The lines are fallen unto me in pleasant places; yea, I have a goodly heritage" (Ps. 16:6). It is as if he says, "No lot ever fell in a better land. My portion falls in the best place that is possible. My knowledge of Thee and interest in Thee affords full content and felicity to me. I have enough, and crave no more. I have all, and can have no more."

If it were possible for one man to be crowned with the royal diadem and dominion of the whole world, and to enjoy all the treasures, honors, and pleasures that all the kingdoms on earth can yield, and if his senses and understanding were enlarged to the utmost of created capacity to taste and take in whatever comfort and delight the universe can give, and if he were to enjoy the society of glorious angels and glorified saints thrown into the bargain, and if he were to enjoy all these things the whole length of the world's duration, yet, without God, this man would be unsatisfied. These things, like dew, may wet the branches (please the flesh), but leave the root dry (the spirit discontented).

However, if the same man were to see God, and if God were to possess his heart, then his infinite desires would expire in the bosom of his Maker. Without this river of paradise, there is such a drought in the heart of man that not all the waters in the world, even if every drop were an ocean, can quench it. Oh, what dry chips are all creatures to a hungry immortal soul! "Lord," says Augustine, "Thou hast made our heart for Thee, and it will never rest till it come to Thee; and when I shall wholly cleave to Thee, then my life will be lively."

There are two special faculties in man's soul: the understanding and the will. These must be satisfied with suitable and adequate objects, or else the soul, like the sea, cannot rest. The understanding must be satisfied with truth, and the will must be satisfied with good. In an attempt to fill these two faculties, men are as busy as bees, flying over the field of the world, trying every flower for sweetness. Yet, after all their toil and labor, they rest themselves, like wasps, in combs without any honey.

The understanding must be suited with the highest truth, but the world is a lie, and the things in the world are lying vanities. They are not what they seem to be (Jonah 2:8). Therefore, they are unable to satisfy the mind. However, God is eternal truth, and true eternity. All truth is originally in Him. His nature is the idea of truth, and His will is the standard of truth. It is eternal life and utmost satisfaction to know Him, because the understanding is perfected by knowing Him. The soul will see all truth in God—not only clearly, but fully in the other world, where the Christian's happiness will be complete—face-to-face. Aristotle, although a heathen, thought that happiness consisted in the knowledge of the chiefest good. When Archimedes discovered the solution to one mathematical question he was so excited that he ran up and down, crying, "I have found it! I have found it!" How much more will the Christian be transported when he will know all that is knowable, and all shadows of ignorance will vanish as the darkness before the rising sun!

The will must also be satisfied with good. According to the degree of goodness in the object, such is the degree of satisfaction to the faculty. Now, the things of this life, although good in themselves, are vain and evil because of man's sin (Rom. 8:20). They are at best fading and limited good things. For this reason, they are incapable of filling this faculty. As truth is the object of the understanding, so good is the object of the will. Furthermore, that good which satisfies must be the best; otherwise, the soul will still crave more. It must also be perfect; otherwise, it will never fill the soul. God is such a good. He is essentially, universally, unchangeably, and infinitely good, and therefore He satisfies. "I shall be satisfied, when I awake, with thy likeness" (Ps. 17:15). When the morning of the resurrection dawns and the sound of the last trumpet awakens me, oh, my soul will enjoy the sweet satisfaction and ravishing delight in being full of Thy likeness and Thy love!

Before the happiness of a saint appears in full view, it casts, like the rising sun with its forerunning rays, a lightsome, gladsome brightness upon the believer, so that he is filled with joy at present, and would not part with his hopes of it for the whole world. "They shall be abundantly satisfied with the fatness of thy house [while on this side heaven]; and thou shalt make them drink of the river of thy pleasures" (Ps. 36:8). Although the wedding dinner is deferred until the wedding day, the Christian encounters many banquets along the way. He does not merely enjoy pleasures ("fatness of thy house") here below, but plenty of them: "They shall be abundantly satisfied" (Ps. 36:8).

The world is like sharp sauce that fails to fill while provoking the stomach to call for more. However, the infinite God, like solid food, satisfies the soul fully, and causes it to cry out, "I have enough!"

2. God Is a Sanctifying Portion

The world cannot advance the soul in the least. The things of the world are fittingly compared to a man's shadow—no matter how long it is, his body remains the same. So it is with your estate—no matter how great it is, your soul is not any better. The greatest letter adds no more to the meaning of a word than the smallest letter. Men in high places are the same men. No real worth is added to them by virtue of their position.

It is evident that men are actually the worse for their earthly portions. If some were not so wealthy, they would not be so wicked. Most of the world's favorites, like some stomachs, are fuller with appetite than digestion. They eat more than they can digest, resulting in disease. By feeding on the trash of earth, their stomachs are turned off substantial food—the bread of heaven. Aristotle tells us of a sea, where (by virtue of some whirling property) ships are cast away in the midst of calm. Likewise, many perish in their greatest prosperity. They are so busy with toys and rattles that they have no free time to be saved (Luke 14:18).

That which elevates and ennobles the soul of man must be more excellent than the soul. Silver is cheapened by mixing it with lead, but ennobled by mixing it with gold. Why? The former is inferior to it, but the latter excels it. The world, and all that is in it, is infinitely inferior to the soul of man, and therefore it is debased by mingling with them. But God is infinitely superior, and therefore He advances the soul by uniting with it. That coin which is the most excellent metal defiles our hands and is prone to defile our hearts, but the divine nature elevates and purifies the soul.

The best portions of this life are like the cities that Solomon gave to Hiram. "And Hiram came out from Tyre to see the cities which Solomon had given him; and they pleased him not. And he said, What cities are these which thou hast given me, my brother? And he called them the land of Cabul [i.e., dirty or displeasing] unto this day" (1 Kings 9:12–13). The most pleasant portion in this world lies in the land of Cabul It is dirty and displeasing. It both defiles and dissatisfies. However, the heavenly portion, like honey, both delights and cleanses, both pleases and purifies.

Outward things, like common stones to a ring, add nothing at all to the worth of the soul. However, this sparkling diamond, this pearl of great price, the infinite God, makes the gold ring of the soul to be of unspeakable value. "The heart of the wicked is little worth" (Prov. 10:20). His house is worth something, but his heart is worth nothing, because it is a ditch full of dirt. His earthly portion possesses his heart. However, the heart of a godly man is worth millions, because it is the cabinet in which this inestimable jewel is stored. "The righteous is more excellent than his neighbor" (Prov. 12:26), because he partakes of the divine nature. God, like gold, enriches whatever He unites Himself to. Hence it is that things which excel in Scripture are usually said to be things of God; e.g., the garden of God (Ezek. 28:13), the hill of God (Ps. 68:15), the mountains of God (Ps. 36:6), the city of God (John 3:3), the cedars of God (Ps. 80:10)—that is, the most excellent garden, hill, mountain, city, and cedars.

God is the perfection of your soul. Thus if He were your portion, He would advance your soul. Oh, what a height of honor and happiness would you experience if this God were yours! At present, like a worm, you crawl on, and dwell in, the earth—the meanest and basest of all the elements, which brutes trample under their feet. However, then, like an eagle, you would mount up to heaven, condemning these toys, and leaving these trifles for children. You would, as an angel, always stand in the presence of God, and enjoy unspeakable pleasure in Him, who is your portion. Your life at present is low, differing little from the life of a beast, consisting chiefly in making provision for the flesh (that which should be your slave). Then your life would be high and noble, resembling the lives of those honorable servants, whose continual practice is to adore and admire the blessed and only potentate.

Do you not find by experience that earthly things obstruct holiness, thereby hindering your soul's happiness? Alas, the best of them are like the wings of a butterfly, which, though wonderfully painted, foul the fingers! However, if your heart were to close with God as your portion, it would become purer and nearer to perfection every day. Perhaps you have much gold and silver. The Midianites' camels had chains of gold (Judg. 8:26). Were they any better for it? Many brutes have silver bells, but their natures remain brutish. However, oh, the excellence that God would add to your soul by bestowing upon it His own likeness and love, if you were to take Him as your portion!

CHAPTER 19

God Gives Joy
in Full and Forever

3. God Is a Universal Portion

God has all good things eminently and infinitely in Himself. Creatures are limited in their beings, and therefore limited in the comfort they can provide. Health answers sickness, but it does not answer poverty. Honor is a help against disgrace, but not against pain. Money is the universal medicine, and therefore it is said to answer all things. However, as great a monarch as money is, it cannot command ease in sickness or honor in disgrace—nor can it heal a wounded soul. At best, creatures are particular beings and so particular blessings. Now, man is a collection of many wants and weaknesses. Therefore, he can never be happy until he finds an ointment for every sore—a remedy that is equal to the number and nature of his ailments.

Ahab, sitting upon his throne of glory in his ivory palace, attended by his noble lords, and swaying a large scepter, was miserable because the heavens were brass (1 Kings. 18:1–2). Haman, although he had the favor of the king, the adoration of the people, and the sway over a hundred and twenty-seven provinces, was discontent because he wanted Mordecai's knee (Esth. 3:5). The world's darlings enjoy many good things. Yet their lack of one thing, as Christ told the young man (Mark 10:21), means they lose everything.

However, God is all good things, and every good thing. He is self-sufficient, alone sufficient, and all sufficient. Nothing is lacking in Him—either for the soul's protection from all evil, or for the soul's perfection with all good. Reader, if God were your portion, you would find in Him whatever your heart could desire and whatever could lead you to happiness! Are you ambitious? God is a crown of glory, and a royal diadem. Are you covetous? God is unsearchable riches, yes, durable riches, and righteousness. Are you lustful? God is rivers of pleasures and fullness of joy. Are you hungry? God is a feast of wine on the lees and of fat things full of marrow. Are you weary? God is rest—a shadow from the heat and a shelter from the storm. Are you weak? God is everlasting strength. Are you in doubts? God is marvelous in counsel. Are you in darkness? God is the Sun of righteousness, an eternal light. Are you sick? He is the God of your health. Are you sorrowful? He is the God of all consolations. Are you dying? He is the fountain and God of life. Are you in any distress? His name is a strong tower, to which you may run to find safety. He is a universal medicine against all sorts of miseries.

Whatever your calamity, He can remove it. Whatever your necessity, He can relieve it. He is silver, gold, honor, delight, food, raiment, house, land, peace, wisdom, power, beauty, father, mother, wife, husband, mercy, love, grace, glory, and infinitely more than all these!

God, and all His creatures, are no more than God without any of His creatures. What the Jews say of manna (that it had all sorts of delicate tastes in it) is most true of God. He has all sorts of delights in Him. This tree of life bears twelve manners of fruit every month (Rev. 22:2). In it, there is both variety and plenty of comforts. Its variety prevents our loathing, whereas its plenty prevents our lacking.

A man, desirous to see the famous city of Athens, was told, "See but Solon, and in him you will see all the rarities and excellencies of Athens." Reader, would you like to see all the wealth and worth of sea and land? Would you like to be on the pinnacle of the temple, as Christ was, and have all the kingdoms of the world offered to you? Would you like to view heaven's glorious city, the royal palace of the great King, its costly, curious workmanship, and its unimaginable rarities and delights, which infinite wisdom devised, infinite power and love erected, and infinite bounty enriched? You may both see and enjoy all this in God. If you see but God, you see all! If you enjoy but God, you enjoy all in Him!

A merchant in London may import the horses of Barbary, the sacks of Canary, the wines of France, the sweets of Spain, the oils of Candia, the spices of Egypt, the artificial wares of Alexandria, the silks of Persia, the embroideries of Turkey, the golden wedges of India, the emeralds of Scythia, the topazes of Ethiopia, and the diamonds of Bisnager. Likewise, you, if this God is your portion, may bring in the finest bread to feed you, the choicest wine to comfort you, oil to cheer you, joy to refresh you, raiment to clothe you, the jewels of grace to beautify you, and the crown of glory to make you blessed. All the wealth of this and the other world are yours. All the riches in the covenant of grace, all the good things that Christ purchased with His precious blood, as much good as is in an infinite God—you can have it!

This one God can fill up your soul to its utmost capacity. It is such an end that, when you attain it, you cannot go any farther, and you cannot desire any more. You quietly rest forever. The universality of good in this one God proclaims His infinite worth. There are all perfections in this one God. What a portion is this friend!

4. God Is an Eternal Portion

The pleasures of sin are but for a season—a little inch of time. A season is a very short space, but the portion of a saint is forever. "God is the strength of my heart, and my portion forever" (Ps. 73:26). The greatest estate here below is a flood that soon rises and falls. However, if God says to your soul, as to Aaron's, "I am thine inheritance" (Num. 18:20), neither men nor devils can take it from you. "The LORD knoweth the days of the upright; and their inheritance shall be forever" (Ps. 37:18).

The prodigal wasted his portion, and thus came to poverty (Luke 15:14). The glutton swallows down his portion, burying it in his belly. The drunkard vomits up his portion. The ambitious person often turns his portion into smoke, and it vanishes in the air. Those whose portion continues the longest, will still lose it when death comes with a command from heaven to eject them. All these portions are dying gourds, deceitful brooks, and flying shadows.

Yet how contrary to this is the believer's portion! God is an eternal portion. If He were your portion, He would be your portion forever! When your estate, children, wife, honors, and all earthly things are taken from you, He is the good part that will never be taken from you (Luke 10:42). Your friends may use you as a suit of apparel, which, when they have worn it out, they throw it away, and look for a new one. Your relations may serve you as women use their flowers; they stick them in their bosoms when fresh and flourishing; but, when dying and withered, they throw them on the dunghill. Your riches, honors, pleasures, wife, and children, may stand on the shore and see you launching into the ocean of eternity, but they will not set one foot in the water after you. Only this God is your portion. He will never leave you nor forsake you (Heb. 13:5).

Oh, how happy would you be to have such a friend!

Your portion would be tied to you in this life. It would be impossible to sever it from you. The world could not do it, for you would live above the world while you walk in it. You would behave in it, not as its champion, but its conqueror. "Whatsoever is born of God, overcometh the world" (1 John 5:4). Satan could not separate you from your portion. Your God has him in His chain. Although he may bark, like a watchdog without teeth, he can never bite or hurt God's children. "I write unto you, young men, because ye have overcome the wicked one" (1 John 2:13). You could not even sell away your portion, because you would be a joint-heir with Christ. Coheirs cannot sell unless both agree. However, Christ knows the worth of this inheritance too well to part with it for all that this beggarly world can give (Rom. 8:17).

The apostle makes a challenge which men and devils could never accept: "Who shall separate us from the love of Christ? shall tribulation, or distress, or persecution, or famine, or nakedness, or sword? Nay, in all these things we are more than conquerors through him that loved us" (Rom. 8:35, 37). At death, your portion will swim out with you from the shipwreck, which parts all other portions from men. Then, and not until then, you will know what it is worth. Even at the great day, the fire that will consume the world will not so much as singe your portion. You may stand upon its ruins and sing, "I have lost nothing. I have my portion, my inheritance, my happiness, my God!"

Other portions, like summer fruit, are soon ripe and soon rotten. However, this portion, like winter fruit that is gathered much later, continues. Gold and silver, in which other men's portion are found, are corruptible. However, your portion, like the body of Christ, will never see corruption. All earthly portions, as water in cisterns, quickly grow unsavory. However, this portion is incapable of spoiling.

Oh, friend, what are all the portions in the world (which, like a candle, are consumed in their use and then go out in a stink) in comparison to this eternal portion? It is reported of one Theodorus that, when there was music and feasting in his father's house, he withdrew from all the festivities and thought to himself, "Here is enough pleasure for the flesh, but how long will it last? It will not last for long." Then, falling on his knees, he cried, "Oh Lord, my heart is open to Thee. I do not know what to ask, but only this, Lord, let me not die eternally! O Lord, Thou knowest I love Thee! Oh, let me live eternally to praise Thee!"

I must tell you, reader, that to be eternally happy or eternally miserable, to live eternally or to die eternally, are of greater importance than you are aware. They are of far more concernment than you can conceive. Ponder this motive, therefore, thoroughly: God is not only a satisfying portion, filling every crevice of your soul with the light of joy and comfort, and a sanctifying portion, elevating your soul to its primitive and original perfection, and a universal portion (not health, wealth, friends, honors, liberty, life, house, wife, child, pardon, peace, grace, glory, earth, or heaven), but He is an eternal portion. This God can be your God forever and ever (Ps. 48:14). Oh, sweet word, forever! Thou art the crown of the saints' crown, and the glory of their glory!

Their portion is so full that they desire no more. They enjoy variety and plenty of delights above what they are able to ask or think. They want nothing but to have it fixed. They will trample all the kingdoms of the earth as dirt under their feet, in order to possess it in peace without interruption or cessation. The welcome dove that brings this olive branch in its mouth is this: God is our God forever and ever. All the mathematical figures of days, months, years, and ages, are nothing to this infinite term, forever. Although it stands for nothing in the popular account, yet it contains all our millions—yes, our millions and millions of millions are less than drops in this ocean forever!

If all the pleasures of the whole creation cannot counteract the fruition of God, not even for one moment, how happy would you be to enjoy Him forever! If the first fruits and foretastes of the Christian's felicity are so ravishing, what will the harvest be? Friend, you think but little of what crowns, scepters, palms, thrones, kingdoms, glories, beauties, banquets, angelical entertainments, beatific visions, societies, varieties, and eternities are prepared for those who choose God for their portion. If the saint's cross, in the judgment of Moses—when old enough to make a true estimate of things—was more worth than all the treasures of Egypt (Heb. 11:26), what is the saint's crown, eternal crown, worth?

To conclude this use, reader, take a serious view of the portion that is here offered to you. Consider upon what easy terms it may be yours forever. This portion is no less than the infinite God is. "Behold, the nations are as a drop of the bucket, and are counted as the small dust of the balance…all nations before him are as nothing, and they are counted to him less than nothing, and vanity" (Isa. 40:15, 17). Other portions are bodily, but He is spiritual, and so suitable to your soul. Other portions are mixed, but He is pure. There is not the least spot in this Sun. He is a sea of sweetness without the smallest drop of gall. Other portions are particular—there are some chinks in the outward man that they cannot fill, and there are many leaks in the inner man that they cannot stop. However, God is a universal portion.

All the excellencies of the creatures, even when their imperfections are removed, are but dark shadows in comparison to the substantial excellencies that are in Him. He made all, He has all, and He is all. The most fluent tongue is quickly at a loss in extolling Him, for He is above all blessing and praise. Other portions are debasing, like dross to gold, but He is an advancing portion, as a set of diamonds to a royal crown, infinitely adding to its value. Other portions are perishing. They may be lost. They will be left behind when death calls. Your cloth will then be drawn, and not one dish will remain on the table. Nevertheless, God is an everlasting portion. The soul that feasts with Him, like Mephibosheth at David's table (2 Sam. 11:13), eats bread at His table continually. "In thy presence is fullness of joy; at thy right hand there are pleasures forevermore" (Ps. 16:11). Now, is this not infinite reason why you should choose this God for your portion?

Consider the terms upon which He is willing to be your portion. He desires no more than that you take Him for your treasure and happiness. Surely, such a portion is worthy of all acceptance. Be your own judge—may not God expect, and does not God deserve, as much respect as your earthly portion had? Can your esteem for Him be too high, or your love for Him be too hot, or your labor for Him be too great? Oh, what warm embraces you have given the world! Throw that wench out of your arms, and take the fairest of ten thousand in her place! What high thoughts you have had of the world! What would you have done or suffered to have gained a little more of it? Now, pull down that usurper out of the throne, and set the King of saints there. Esteem Him superlatively above all things, and make it your business, whatever He calls you to do or suffer, to gain His love, which is infinitely better than life itself. If you exalt Him in your heart as your chiefest good, and in your life as your utmost end, then He will give Himself to you.

Is it not rational what He desires? Why would you refuse Him? Here is God; there is the world. Here is bread; there are husks. Here is the substance; there is a shadow. Here is Paradise; there is an apple. Here is fullness; there is emptiness. Here is a fountain; there is a broken cistern. Here is all things; there is nothing. Here is heaven; there is hell. Here is eternity of joy and pleasure; there is eternity of sorrow and pain! Choose which one you will take. "Advise thyself what word I shall bring to him that sent me" (1 Chron. 21:12).

CHAPTER 20

Take Comfort

Finally, this doctrine is useful by way of consolation. It provides comfort to every true Christian. Your portion is not in toys and trifles, or in limited creatures, but in the blessed and boundless God. He who has my lord mayor as his friend cannot be poor—much less he who has God as his portion. It is a portion so precious and perfect that none of the greatest mathematicians can compute its worth. It is a portion so permanent that neither death, nor life, nor the world, nor principalities, nor powers, nor things present, nor things to come, can separate you from it (Rom. 8:38–39). This pleasant thought is able to enliven you in a dying state—nothing can separate you and your portion. The winter can freeze the ponds, but not the ocean. All other portions are frozen and useless in hard weather, but this portion is always full and filling. Hagar wept when her bottle of water was empty (Gen. 21:19), because she did not see the fountain that was so near her. The absence of the creatures should not cause you to mourn, for you have the presence of the Creator.

You can derive comfort from your portion in the most afflicted condition. Do men plunder your estate? You are rich in God, and can joyfully endure the spoiling of your goods, knowing that you have a more enduring substance (Heb. 10:34). Do they cast you into prison? Although your body is in chains, your soul enjoys freedom. No chains can prevent you from mounting up to heaven upon the wings of meditation and prayer. Do they take away your food? You have food to eat that they know nothing about, and you have wine to drink that gladdens man's heart (Ps. 104:15). Is your body sick? Your soul is sound and, as long as it is, all is well. Is your life in danger? If your enemies kill you, they cannot hurt you. On the contrary, they do you the greatest courtesy. They perform that kindness for which you have prayed and sighed on many occasions—to be free from your corruptions, and to behold the blissful vision. When they call you out to die, they do, as Christ to Peter (Matt. 17:1–9), call you up the mount to see your Savior transfigured. Moreover, you will say, "Oh, it is good to be here!"

The Christian can rejoice under the greatest outward misery. What weight can sink him who has the everlasting arms to support him? What need can sadden him who has infinite bounty and mercy to supply him? Nothing can make him miserable, for he has God for his happiness. "Blessed is the nation whose God is the Lord"

(Ps. 33:12). Oh Christian, you can walk in such a manner that the world knows that you are above their threatening and that all their allurements are below your hopes.

Now, this doctrine is a particular comfort in the face of death. First, it is a comfort against the death of our Christian friends. God is a godly man's portion. Therefore, our friends who die in the Lord are blessed. In addition, we who live in the Lord are blessed. It is a comfort to know that they are happy without creatures. What wise man will grieve at his friend's gain? In the ceremonial law, there was a year of jubilee, in which every man who had lost or sold his land, gained it back. The day of death for your believing friend is his day of jubilee, in which he is restored to the possession of his eternal and inestimable portion. Who complains about receiving his inheritance once he comes of age? Their death is not penal, but remedial. It is not destructive, but perfective to their souls. It does for them what none of the ordinances of God, the providences of God, or graces of the Spirit, ever did for them. It sends the weary soul to its sweet and eternal rest. This serpent is turned into a rod (Ex. 4:3–4), with which God works wonders for their good.

The Thracians wept at the births of men, and feasted at their funerals. Why? They counted mortality a mercy, because they viewed death as the end of their outward sufferings. Will not we, who see death as the beginning of matchless and endless solace, rejoice? A wife may well wring her hands, and pierce her heart with sorrow, when her husband is taken away from her, and dragged to hell. However, surely she may rejoice when he is called from her by his Prince to live at court in the greatest honors and pleasures, especially when she is promised within a few days to join him and share with him in those joys and delights forever.

Some observe that, when Jacob died, the Egyptians mourned longer than Joseph did. The reason is this: all their hope was in this life. However, Joseph knew that his father's soul was translated to the heavenly Canaan, just as his body was carried to the earthly Canaan. "I would not have you to be ignorant, brethren, concerning them which are asleep, that ye sorrow not, even as others which have no hope" (1 Thess. 4:13).

As they are happy without us, so we are happy without them. We still have our God. The stormy wind that blew out our candles did not extinguish our sun. When on his or her deathbed, our friend may say to us, as Jacob to his sons, "I die: and God will surely visit you" (Gen. 50:24). "I will never leave thee, nor forsake thee" (Heb. 13:5). Reader, I hope you are not lost or undone if your friends die. May not God say to you, when you are pining and whining for the death of your relations or friends as if you were eternally miserable, as Elkanah to Hannah: "Am not I better to thee than ten sons?" (1 Sam. 1:8). Is not God better to you than ten husbands, ten wives, or ten thousand worlds? Oh, think of it, and take comfort in it!

Second, it is a comfort against your death. God is your portion, and at death you will take possession of your vast estate. At present, you have an estate held in law and a right to it. At death, you will have an estate held in deed, and possession of it. It is strange that some unbelievers, who cannot see the joys and pleasures of the other world, or the hopes that alone can make death truly desirable, meet this foe, death, with less fear than many Christians do. At times, it is actually more difficult to persuade such pagans to live out all their days than it is to persuade some Christians to be willing to die when God calls them.

Codrus threw himself into a pit, so that his country might live by his death. Platinus, the philosopher, viewed mortality as a mercy, because it frees men from the miseries of this life. Having read Plato's *Of the Soul's Immortality*, Cleombrotus sent his soul out of his body in an attempt to taste immortality. According to Caesar, the Druids were hardy in danger and fearless in death, because they believed the soul had a continuance after death. Surely, Christians have more cause to be valiant in their last conflict! It is no credit to their Father that they are so reluctant to go home. The Turks maintain that Christians do not believe that heaven is as glorious a place as they claim. If they did, they would not be so unwilling to go there. The child that wanders far from home convinces the world that he receives a cold welcome at his father's house. Certainly, such Christians bring an ill report upon the good land.

Christian, what is it in death that frightens you? Is it not a departure, the jail releasing one who has been imprisoned a long time? Is it not the sleep of your body and the awakening of your soul? Is it not the way to bliss, the gate to life, and the portal to paradise? Are you not certain to overcome death when you leave your body, and to be joined to your head? The Roman general, in the encounter between Scipio and Hannibal, encouraged his soldiers to fight by telling them that they were about to face those whom they had formerly overcome, and those who were as much their slaves as their enemies. You are to enter the battle against that adversary whom you conquered long ago in Jesus Christ, and who is more your slave than your enemy. Death is yours (1 Cor. 3:22). Your servant will help you remove your clothes, and place you in your everlasting, happy rest.

Is it the tearing down of your earthly tabernacle that troubles you? Do you not know that death is the worker sent by the Father to pull down this earthly house of clay and mortality, so that it may be set up anew, infinitely more lasting, beautiful, and glorious? If you were to see how rich and splendid He intends to make it, you would contentedly endure the present toil and trouble, and be thankful to Him for His care and cost. He takes down your vile body that He may fashion it like the glorious body of His own Son, which excels the sun in brightness and beauty.

Is it the untying of the knot between body and soul that perplexes you? It is true that they part, but they do so as friends, going two different ways, shaking hands until they return from their journey. They are as certain of meeting again as of parting. Your soul will return laden with the wealth of heaven, and fetch his old companion to the participation of all his joy and happiness.

Is it the rotting of your body in the grave that grieves you? Indeed, Plato's worldly man sadly bewails it: "Woe is me that I will lie alone rotting in the earth among the crawling worms, not seeing anything above, nor being seen." However, you know that the grave is a sweet bed of spices for your body to rest in. Have you never heard God speaking to you, as once to Jacob, "Fear not to go down into Egypt [into the grave]...for I will go down with thee...and I will also surely bring thee up again" (Gen. 46:3–4)?

Besides, your soul will never die. The heathen historian comforted himself against death with this weak medicine, "Not all of me dies. Although my body is mortal, my books are immortal." However, you have a richer medicine to clear your souls. When your body fails, your soul flourishes. Your death is a burnt offering. When your ashes fall to the earth, the celestial flame of your soul mounts up to heaven. In addition, death relieves you of the most troublesome guests that make your life so burdensome. As the fire to the three young men did not so much as singe or sear their bodies, but burned and consumed their bonds (Dan. 2:23–27), so death will not hurt your body or soul in the least, but it will destroy those fetters of sin and sorrow, in which you are entangled.

Furthermore, at death, your soul will enjoy the sight of the blessed God, which is the only beatific vision. Popish pilgrims take tedious journeys and experience much expense and hardship in order to behold a dumb idol. The queen of Sheba came from far to see Solomon and hear his wisdom (1 Kings 10:1). Moreover, will you not take a step from earth to heaven to see Jesus Christ, who is greater than Solomon is? In a moment, in the twinkling of an eye, your journey will be done, and your work will be done. Have you not prayed and cried for it on many occasions? Have you not trembled with the thought that you may miss it? Has your heart not leaped with joy repeatedly in hope of it? In addition, when the hour comes, and you are sent for, do you shrink back? You should be ashamed, Christian! Walk worthy of your calling, and quicken your courage in your last conflict!

When it thunders, the Jews open their windows, expecting the Messiah to come. Oh, when the storm of death beats upon your body, with what joy may you open wide those windows of your soul—faith and hope! You know that your dearest Redeemer, who went before you to prepare a place for you, will then come and receive you to Himself, that where He is, there you may be also—forever (John 14:2–3)!

Some other
Puritan Resources

from
**REFORMATION
HERITAGE BOOKS**

"Trading and Thriving in Godliness": The Piety of George Swinnock

Edited and Introduced by J. Stephen Yuille

978-1-60178-041-6   Paperback, 235 pages

In *"Trading and Thriving in Godliness,"* J. Stephen Yuille highlights George Swinnock's conviction that godliness is the primary employment of every Christian. Yuille begins the book by analyzing the influences on, groundwork for, and expressions of piety in Swinnock's life and thought. The remainder of the book presents fifty selections from Swinnock's writings that exemplify his teaching on the foundation, value, pursuit, nature, and means of godliness, as well as its motives.

"Swinnock gives us the essence of Puritanism and J. Stephen Yuille gives us the essence of Swinnock. Here is doctrine and life, vision and devotion, the poetry and the passion of typical Puritan preaching. A first-rate taster of what is available in Swinnock's *Works*."

— Peter Lewis, author of *The Genius of Puritanism*

Meet the Puritans

Joel R. Beeke and Randall J. Pederson

978-1-60178-000-3   Hardback, 935 pages

Meet the Puritans provides a biographical and theological introduction to the Puritans whose works have been reprinted in the last fifty years, and also gives helpful summaries and insightful analyses of those reprinted works. It contains nearly 150 biographical entries, and nearly 700 summaries of reprinted works. A very useful resource for getting into the Puritans.

> "As furnaces burn with ancient coal and not with the leaves that fall from today's trees, so my heart is kindled with the fiery substance I find in the old Scripture-steeped sermons of Puritan pastors. A warm thanks to the authors of *Meet the Puritans* for all the labor to make them known."
>
> —John Piper, Pastor,
> Bethlehem Baptist Church,
> Minneapolis, Minnesota

The Path of True Godliness

Willem Teellinck

Translated by Annemie Godbehere
Edited by Joel R. Beeke

978-1-892777-75-1   Paperback, 303 pages

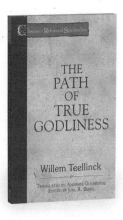

Willem Teellinck (1579–1629) assists the reader in developing the character of true godliness and standing guard against the kingdom of darkness that opposes it. By mapping out the means to and motivations for the practice of godliness, this old Dutch writer provides us with one of the best books ever written on sanctification.

"I am delighted that the Dutch Reformed Translation Society is making this material available in the English language. It is a landmark feature of our Reformed heritage, and it is rich food for the soul in this or any other age."

—J. I. Packer, author of
*A Quest for Godliness: The Puritan
Vision of the Christian Life*

Heirs with Christ:
The Puritans on Adoption

Joel R. Beeke

978-1-60178-040-9   Hardcover, 160 pages

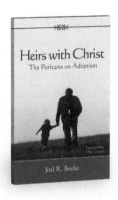

The Puritans have gotten bad press for their supposed lack of teaching on the doctrine of spiritual adoption. In *Heirs with Christ*, Joel R. Beeke dispels this caricature and shows that the Puritan era did more to advance the idea that every true Christian is God's adopted child than any other age of church history. This little book lets the Puritans speak for themselves, showing how they recognized adoption's far-reaching, transforming power and comfort for the children of God.

"More than just historically informative, this volume should be warmly welcomed by all Christians who want to learn more about this crucial aspect of our identity as sons of God and joint-heirs with Christ."

— Justin Taylor, co-editor with John Piper
of *A God Entranced Vision of All Things:
The Legacy of Jonathan Edwards*

The Inner Sanctum of Puritan Piety:
John Flavel's Doctrine of Mystical Union with Christ

J. Stephen Yuille

978-1-60178-017-1   Paperback, 140 pages

In *The Inner Sanctum of Puritan Piety*, J. Stephen Yuille demonstrates how the doctrine of the believer's union with Christ lies at the heart of the Puritan pursuit of godliness. He analyzes the whole corpus of Flavel's writing, showing how this mystical union is set upon the backdrop of God's covenant of redemption and established on the basis of the person and work of Jesus Christ. Chapters on the nature and acts of this union help readers gain a better understanding of what this union is, while chapters on the blessings, fruit, suffering, evidence, joy, practice, and hope associated with this union show more fully the experiential direction of Flavel's approach to theology.

> "This study of John Flavel on union with Christ is indeed a welcome one!"
>
> — Michael A. G. Haykin, Professor of Church History and Biblical Spirituality at Southern Baptist Theological Seminary